Wonderful ways to prepare

CHINESE
DISHES

by JO ANN SHIRLEY

TITLES IN THIS SERIES

Wonderful ways to prepare

CHINESE
DISHES

PLAYMORE INC. NEW YORK USA
UNDER ARRANGEMENT WITH
WALDMAN PUBLISHING CORP.

AYERS & JAMES
SYDNEY AUSTRALIA

STAFFORD PEMBERTON PUBLISHING
KNUTSFORD UNITED KINGDOM

FIRST PUBLISHED 1979

PUBLISHED IN THE USA
BY PLAYMORE INC.
UNDER ARRANGEMENT WITH
WALDMAN PUBLISHING CORP.

PUBLISHED IN AUSTRALIA
BY AYERS & JAMES
CROWS NEST. AUSTRALIA

PUBLISHED IN THE UNITED KINGDOM
BY STAFFORD PEMBERTON PUBLISHING
KNUTSFORD CHESHIRE

COPYRIGHT © 1979
AYERS & JAMES
5 ALEXANDER STREET
CROWS NEST N.S.W. AUSTRALIA

ISBN 0 86908 153 5

OVEN TEMPERATURE GUIDE

Description	Gas		Electric		Mark
	C	F	C	F	
Cool	100	200	110	225	¼
Very Slow	120	250	120	250	½
Slow	150	300	150	300	1-2
Moderately slow	160	325	170	340	3
Moderate	180	350	200	400	4
Moderately hot	190	375	220	425	5-6
Hot	200	400	230	450	6-7
Very hot	230	450	250	475	8-9

LIQUID MEASURES

IMPERIAL	METRIC
1 teaspoon	5 ml
1 tablespoon	20 ml
2 fluid ounces (½ cup)	62.5 ml
4 fluid ounces (½ cup)	125 ml
8 fluid ounces (1 cup)	250 ml
1 pint (16 ounces — 2 cups)*	500 ml

* (The imperial pint is equal to 20 fluid ounces.)

SOLID MEASURES

AVOIRDUPOIS	METRIC
1 ounce	30 g
4 ounces (¼ lb)	125 g
8 ounces (½ lb)	250 g
12 ounces (¾ lb)	375 g
16 ounces (1 lb)	500 g
24 ounces (1½ lb)	750 g
32 ounces (2 lb)	1000 g (1 kg)

CUP AND SPOON REPLACEMENTS FOR OUNCES

INGREDIENT	½ oz	1 oz	2 oz	3 oz	4 oz	5 oz	6 oz	7 oz	8 oz
Almonds, ground	2 T	¼ C	½ C	¾ C	1¼ C	1⅓ C	1⅔ C	2 C	2¼ C
slivered	6 t	¼ C	½ C	¾ C	1 C	1⅓ C	1⅔ C	2 C	2¼ C
whole	2 T	¼ C	⅓ C	½ C	¾ C	1 C	1¼ C	1⅓ C	1½ C
Apples, dried whole	3 T	½ C	1 C	1⅓ C	2 C	2⅓ C	2¾ C	3⅓ C	3¾ C
Apricots, chopped	2 T	¼ C	½ C	¾ C	1 C	1¼ C	1½ C	1¾ C	2 C
whole	2 T	3 T	½ C	⅔ C	1 C	1¼ C	1⅓ C	1½ C	1¾ C
Arrowroot	1 T	2 T	⅓ C	½ C	⅔ C	¾ C	1 C	1¼ C	1⅓ C
Baking Powder	1 T	2 T	⅓ C	½ C	⅔ C	¾ C	1 C	1 C	1¼ C
Baking Soda	1 T	2 T	⅓ C	½ C	⅔ C	¾ C	1 C	1 C	1¼ C
Barley	1 T	2 T	¼ C	½ C	⅔ C	¾ C	1 C	1 C	1¼ C
Breadcrumbs, dry	2 T	¼ C	½ C	¾ C	1 C	1¼ C	1½ C	1¾ C	2 C
soft	¼ C	½ C	1 C	1½ C	2 C	2½ C	3 C	3⅔ C	4¼ C
Biscuit Crumbs	2 T	¼ C	½ C	¾ C	1¼ C	1⅓ C	1⅔ C	2 C	2¼ C
Butter	3 t	6 t	¼ C	⅓ C	½ C	⅔ C	¾ C	1 C	1 C
Cheese, grated, lightly packed,									
natural cheddar	6 t	¼ C	½ C	¾ C	1 C	1¼ C	1½ C	1¾ C	2 C
Processed cheddar	5 t	2 T	⅓ C	⅔ C	¾ C	1 C	1¼ C	1½ C	1⅔ C
Parmesan, Romano	6 t	¼ C	½ C	¾ C	1 C	1⅓ C	1⅔ C	2 C	2¼ C
Cherries, candied, chopped	1 T	2 T	⅓ C	½ C	¾ C	1 C	1 C	1⅓ C	1½ C
whole	1 T	2 T	⅓ C	½ C	⅔ C	¾ C	1 C	1¼ C	1⅓ C
Cocoa	2 T	¼ C	½ C	¾ C	1¼ C	1⅓ C	1⅔ C	2 C	2¼ C
Coconut, desiccated	2 T	⅓ C	⅔ C	1 C	1⅓ C	1⅔ C	2 C	2⅓ C	2⅔ C
shredded	⅓ C	⅔ C	1¼ C	1¾ C	2½ C	3 C	3⅔ C	4⅓ C	5 C
Cornstarch	6 t	3 T	½ C	⅔ C	1 C	1¼ C	1½ C	1⅔ C	2 C
Corn Syrup	2 t	1 T	2 T	¼ C	⅓ C	½ C	½ C	⅔ C	⅔ C
Coffee, ground	2 T	⅓ C	⅔ C	1 C	1⅓ C	1⅔ C	2 C	2⅓ C	2⅔ C
instant	3 T	½ C	1 C	1⅓ C	1¾ C	2¼ C	2⅔ C	3 C	3½ C
Cornflakes	½ C	1 C	2 C	3 C	4¼ C	5¼ C	6¼ C	7⅓ C	8⅓ C
Cream of Tartar	1 T	2 T	⅓ C	½ C	⅔ C	¾ C	1 C	1 C	1¼ C
Currants	1 T	2 T	⅓ C	⅔ C	¾ C	1 C	1¼ C	1½ C	1⅔ C
Custard Powder	6 t	3 T	½ C	⅔ C	1 C	1¼ C	1½ C	1⅔ C	2 C
Dates, chopped	1 T	2 T	⅓ C	⅔ C	¾ C	1 C	1¼ C	1½ C	1⅔ C
whole, pitted	1 T	2 T	⅓ C	½ C	¾ C	1 C	1¼ C	1⅓ C	1½ C
Figs, chopped	1 T	2 T	⅓ C	½ C	¾ C	1 C	1 C	1⅓ C	1½ C
Flour, all-purpose or cake	6 t	¼ C	½ C	¾ C	1 C	1¼ C	1½ C	1¾ C	2 C
wholemeal	6 t	3 T	½ C	⅔ C	1 C	1¼ C	1⅓ C	1⅔ C	1¾ C
Fruit, mixed	1 T	2 T	⅓ C	½ C	¾ C	1 C	1¼ C	1⅓ C	1½ C
Gelatin	5 t	2 T	⅓ C	½ C	¾ C	1 C	1 C	1¼ C	1½ C
Ginger, crystallised pieces	1 T	2 T	⅓ C	½ C	¾ C	1 C	1¼ C	1⅓ C	1½ C
ground	6 t	⅓ C	½ C	¾ C	1¼ C	1½ C	1¾ C	2 C	2¼ C
preserved, heavy syrup	1 T	2 T	⅓ C	½ C	⅔ C	¾ C	1 C	1 C	1¼ C
Glucose, liquid	2 t	1 T	2 T	¼ C	⅓ C	½ C	½ C	⅔ C	⅔ C
Haricot Beans	1 T	2 T	⅓ C	½ C	⅔ C	¾ C	1 C	1 C	1¼ C

In this table, t represents teaspoonful, T represents tablespoonful and C represents cupful.

CUP AND SPOON REPLACEMENTS FOR OUNCES (Cont.)

INGREDIENT	½ oz	1 oz	2 oz	3 oz	4 oz	5 oz	6 oz	7 oz	8 oz
Honey	2 t	1 T	2 T	¼ C	⅓ C	½ C	½ C	⅔ C	⅔ C
Jam	2 t	1 T	2 T	¼ C	⅓ C	½ C	½ C	⅔ C	¾ C
Lentils	1 T	2 T	⅓ C	½ C	⅔ C	¾ C	1 C	1 C	1¼ C
Macaroni (see pasta)									
Milk Powder, full cream	2 T	¼ C	½ C	¾ C	1¼ C	1⅓ C	1⅔ C	2 C	2¼ C
non fat	2 T	⅓ C	¾ C	1¼ C	1½ C	2 C	2⅓ C	2¾ C	3¼ C
Nutmeg	6 t	3 T	½ C	⅔ C	¾ C	1 C	1¼ C	1½ C	1⅔ C
Nuts, chopped	6 t	¼ C	½ C	¾ C	1 C	1¼ C	1½ C	1¾ C	2 C
Oatmeal	1 T	2 T	½ C	⅔ C	¾ C	1 C	1¼ C	1½ C	1⅔ C
Olives, whole	1 T	2 T	⅓ C	⅔ C	¾ C	1 C	1¼ C	1½ C	1⅔ C
sliced	1 T	2 T	⅓ C	⅔ C	¾ C	1 C	1¼ C	1½ C	1⅔ C
Pasta, short (e.g. macaroni)	1 T	2 T	⅓ C	⅔ C	¾ C	1 C	1¼ C	1½ C	1⅔ C
Peaches, dried & whole	1 T	2 T	⅓ C	⅔ C	¾ C	1 C	1¼ C	1½ C	1⅔ C
chopped	6 t	¼ C	½ C	¾ C	1 C	1¼ C	1½ C	1¾ C	2 C
Peanuts, shelled, raw, whole	1 T	2 T	⅓ C	½ C	¾ C	1 C	1¼ C	1⅓ C	1½ C
roasted	1 T	2 T	⅓ C	⅔ C	¾ C	1 C	1¼ C	1½ C	1⅔ C
Peanut Butter	3 t	6 t	3 T	⅓ C	½ C	½ C	⅔ C	¾ C	1 C
Peas, split	1 T	2 T	⅓ C	½ C	⅔ C	¾ C	1 C	1 C	1¼ C
Peel, mixed	1 T	2 T	⅓ C	½ C	¾ C	1 C	1 C	1¼ C	1½ C
Potato, powder	1 T	2 T	¼ C	⅓ C	½ C	⅔ C	¾ C	1 C	1¼ C
flakes	¼ C	½ C	1 C	1⅓ C	2 C	2⅓ C	2¾ C	3⅓ C	3¾ C
Prunes, chopped	1 T	2 T	⅓ C	½ C	⅔ C	¾ C	1 C	1¼ C	1⅓ C
whole pitted	1 T	2 T	⅓ C	½ C	⅔ C	¾ C	1 C	1 C	1¼ C
Raisins	2 T	¼ C	⅓ C	½ C	¾ C	1 C	1 C	1⅓ C	1½ C
Rice, short grain, raw	1 T	2 T	¼ C	½ C	⅔ C	¾ C	1 C	1 C	1¼ C
long grain, raw	1 T	2 T	⅓ C	½ C	¾ C	1 C	1¼ C	1⅓ C	1½ C
Rice Bubbles	⅔ C	1¼ C	2½ C	3⅔ C	5 C	6¼ C	7½ C	8¾ C	10 C
Rolled Oats	2 T	⅓ C	⅔ C	1 C	1⅓ C	1¾ C	2 C	2½ C	2¾ C
Sago	2 T	¼ C	⅓ C	½ C	¾ C	1 C	1 C	1¼ C	1½ C
Salt, common	3 t	6 t	¼ C	⅓ C	½ C	⅔ C	¾ C	1 C	1 C
Semolina	1 T	2 T	⅓ C	½ C	¾ C	1 C	1 C	1⅓ C	1½ C
Spices	6 t	3 T	¼ C	⅓ C	½ C	½ C	⅔ C	¾ C	1 C
Sugar, plain	3 t	6 t	¼ C	⅓ C	½ C	⅔ C	¾ C	1 C	1 C
confectioners'	1 T	2 T	⅓ C	½ C	¾ C	1 C	1 C	1¼ C	1½ C
moist brown	1 T	2 T	⅓ C	½ C	¾ C	1 C	1 C	1⅓ C	1½ C
Tapioca	1 T	2 T	⅓ C	½ C	⅔ C	¾ C	1 C	1¼ C	1⅓ C
Treacle	2 t	1 T	2 T	¼ C	⅓ C	½ C	½ C	⅔ C	⅔ C
Walnuts, chopped	2 T	¼ C	½ C	¾ C	1 C	1¼ C	1½ C	1¾ C	2 C
halved	2 T	⅓ C	⅔ C	1 C	1¼ C	1½ C	1¾ C	2¼ C	2½ C
Yeast, dried	6 t	3 T	½ C	⅔ C	1 C	1¼ C	1⅓ C	1⅔ C	1¾ C
compressed	3 t	6 t	3 T	⅓ C	½ C	½ C	⅔ C	¾ C	1 C

In this table, t represents teaspoonful, T represents tablespoonful and C represents cupful.

Contents

Soups

Chicken and Corn Soup

1 large chicken breast
½ teaspoon salt
2½ tablespoons cold water
1 can (250 g or 8 oz) creamed
corn
6 cups (1½ liters) chicken
stock

2½ tablespoons cornstarch
1½ teaspoons sesame oil
4 tablespoons Chinese wine
or dry sherry
chopped ham to garnish

1. Remove chicken meat from the bone and mince finely.
2. Mix the chicken with the salt and cold water.
3. Add the creamed corn to the chicken mixture and blend thoroughly.
4. Bring the chicken stock **to a boil**. Add chicken and corn mixture, mix well and return to the boil.
5. Mix cornstarch with a little cold water and add to the soup, stirring constantly. Simmer for about two minutes.
6. Stir in sesame oil and wine or sherry.
7. Garnish with chopped ham just before serving.

Serves 4-6.

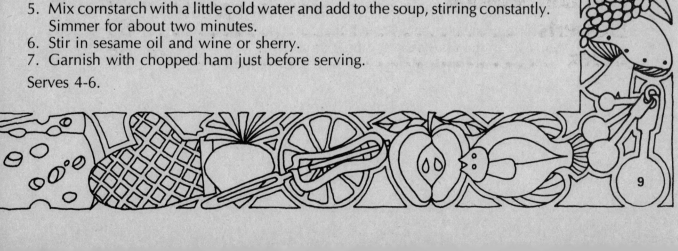

Egg Flower Soup

6 cups (1½ liters) chicken stock	2 teaspoons sesame oil
4 tablespoons Chinese wine or dry sherry	salt
	4 eggs, slightly beaten
	4 scallions, chopped

1. Put stock in a large saucepan and bring to a boil.
2. Add wine or sherry and sesame oil.
3. Season to taste with salt.
4. Slowly add the beaten eggs. Keep the soup boiling while adding the eggs.
5. Garnish with chopped scallions and serve immediately.

Serves 4-6.

Crab and Egg Soup

¼ lb (125 g) canned crabmeat
6 cups (1½ liters) fish stock
5 eggs, slightly beaten
3 tablespoons cornstarch
⅔ cup (165 ml) cold water
5 scallions, chopped

1. Drain liquid from crabmeat.
2. Bring the fish stock to a boil and gradually pour in the beaten eggs stirring constantly. Simmer tor two minutes.
3. Mix the cornstarch with the cold water and add to the soup.
4. Bring the soup back to a boil. Continue stirring until the soup is clear.
5. Mix in the crabmeat and heat thoroughly.
6. Garnish with scallions and serve immediately.

Serves 4-6

Fish and Egg Flower Soup

½ (250 g) fish fillets
4 teaspoons oil
2 teaspoons soy sauce
2 teaspoons cornstarch
½ teaspoon salt

2 eggs
2 teaspoons oil
6 cups (1½ liters) water
2 slices fresh ginger, chopped
4 spring onions, chopped

1. Cut the fish into thin slices.
2. Mix together the 4 teaspoons oil, soy sauce, cornstarch and salt. Marinate the fish slices in this mixture for ½ hour.
3. Beat the eggs with the two teaspoons oil.
4. Put water and ginger into a saucepan and bring to a boil.
5. Add the fish and return to a boil.
6. Add spring onions and slowly stir in the beaten eggs. Add salt to taste and serve immediately.

Serves 4.

Short Soup

¼ lb (125 g) raw shrimp
¼ lb (125 g) minced pork
3 scallions, chopped
½ teaspoon salt
2 tablespoons soy sauce
1 clove garlic, crushed
1 slice fresh ginger,
   finely grated

¼ lb (125 g) won ton wrappers
6 cups (1½ liters) chicken
   stock
¼ teaspoon sesame oil
4 scallions, finely chopped

1. Shell and de-vein the shrimp. Chop finely.
2. Mix the shrimp together with the minced pork, scallions, salt, soy sauce, garlic and ginger.
3. Put a little of the mixture on each won ton wrapper. Fold in two forming a triangle. Moisten the edges and press together. Press all three corners together.
4. Bring the stock to a boil and drop dumplings into it. Cook for about ten minutes.
5. Remove from heat and add sesame oil and scallions. Serve immediately.

Serves 4-6.

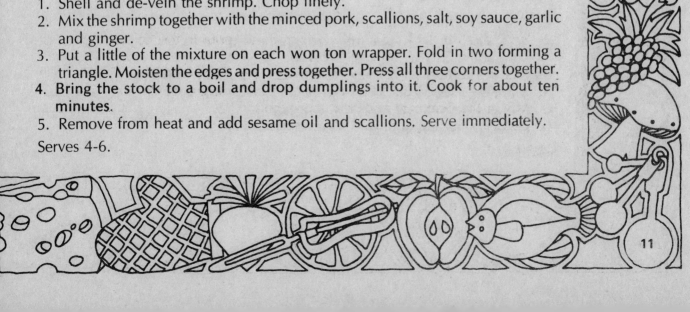

Lettuce and Fish Soup

¼ lb (125 g) fish fillet
1 teaspoon cornstarch
4 teaspoons soy sauce
1 teaspoon sugar
½ teaspoon pepper
4 teaspoons vegetable oil
1 lettuce

2 teaspoons oil
2 slices fresh ginger
2 teaspoons salt
6 cups (1½ liters) boiling water
1½ teaspoons mei-jing powder

1. Cut fish fillet into thin slices. Mix with cornstarch, soy sauce, sugar, pepper and oil.
2. Break off lettuce leaves. Wash, drain and dry thoroughly.
3. Heat two teaspoons of oil in a large saucepan and saute the ginger slice and salt for one minute.
4. Pour in boiling water and bring to a boil.
5. Add lettuce, cover and simmer for five minutes.
6. Add fish and mei-jing powder and simmer for another ten minutes.

Serves 6-8.

Chinese Cabbage Soup

¼ lb (125 g) lean pork
½ teaspoon sugar
¼ teaspoon pepper
2 teaspoons soy sauce
1 teaspoon cornstarch
½ teaspoon sesame oil
2 teaspoons oil

3 slices fresh ginger
4 teaspoons salt
6 cups (1½ liters) boiling water
1 Chinese cabbage
½ teaspoon mei-jing powder

1. Cut pork into thin slices and mix with sugar, pepper, soy sauce, cornstarch and sesame oil.
2. Heat oil in a saucepan and saute the ginger mixed with the salt for one minute.
3. Add boiling water to the ginger.
4. Slice cabbage and add to the soup. Return soup to a boil. Reduce heat, cover and simmer for ten minutes.
5. Stirring constantly, add pork mixture and mei-jing powder. Replace cover and simmer for fifteen minutes.

Serves 6-8

Combination Soup

½ lb (250 g) lean pork or beef
6 cups (1½ liters) water
1 clove garlic, whole
3 slices fresh ginger
2 teaspoons salt
2 stalks celery, chopped
¼ lb (125 g) cooked shrimp

3 cups Chinese cabbage, sliced
¼ lb (125 g) bamboo shoots
4 scallions, roughly chopped
¼ teaspoon sesame oil
2 teaspoons sweet sherry

1. Thinly slice pork or beef.
2. Place meat in a large saucepan with water, garlic, ginger, salt and celery. Bring to a boil. Reduce heat, cover and simmer for about ½ hour. Remove garlic and ginger.
3. If shrimp are large, cut into small pieces. If they are small, keep whole. Add the shrimp to the soup with the cabbage, bamboo shoots and scallions.
4. Bring soup back to a boil and cook for two minutes.
5. Add sesame oil and sherry and serve immediately.

Serves 4-6.

Asparagus and Chicken Soup

8 cups (2 liters) chicken stock
1 large chicken breast
1 bunch fresh asparagus
4 teaspoons cornstarch
3 tablespoons cold water
2½ tablespoons dry sherry
2 eggs, beaten

1. Heat the chicken stock in a large saucepan.
2. Remove the meat from the bone and cut into small pieces.
3. Wash asparagus well, cut off hard stems and cook in boiling salted water until tender. When cooked, cut into small pieces. Set aside. Reserve liquid from saucepan.
4. Add one cup of asparagus liquid to chicken stock.
5. Add chicken and bring to the boil. Reduce heat and simmer for ten minutes.
6. Mix cornstarch with the cold water and add to the soup, stirring constantly.
7. Add sherry.
8. Slowly add beaten eggs and asparagus pieces. Heat thoroughly.

Serves 4-6.

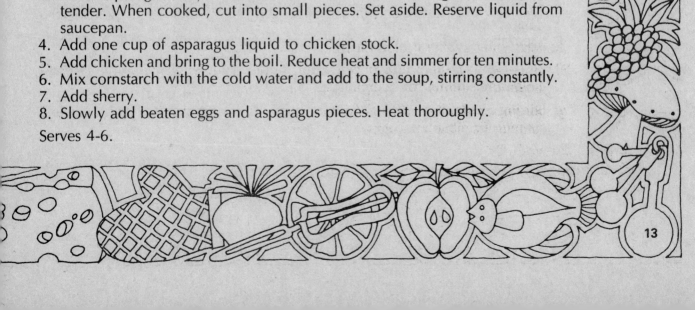

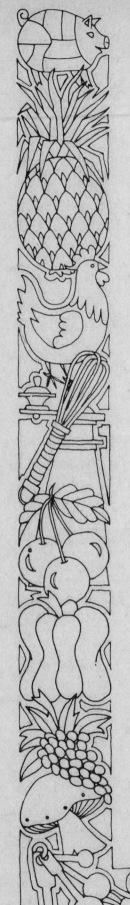

Watercress Soup

¼ lb (125 g) lean pork
1½ teaspoons cornstarch
½ teaspoon sugar
½ teaspoon pepper
2 tablespoons soy sauce
2 tablespoons oil

2 slices fresh ginger
4 teaspoons salt
6 cups (1½ liters) boiling
water
1 lb (500 g) watercress

1. Cut the pork into thin slices. Mix with cornstarch, sugar, pepper, soy sauce and one tablespoon oil.
2. Heat the remaining oil in a saucepan and saute the ginger and salt for one minute.
3. **Pour in the boiling water and bring to a boil.**
4. Add watercress, cover and simmer for five minutes.
5. Gently stir in the pork mixture, replace lid and simmer for another fifteen minutes.

Serves 6-8.

Chicken Liver Soup

½ lb (250 g) chicken livers
2 tablespoons soy sauce
½ teaspoon sugar
1½ teaspoons cornstarch
2 tablespoons oil
½ teaspoon pepper

2 slices fresh ginger
2 teaspoons salt
6 cups (1½ liters) boiling
water
1 lb (500 g) spinach

1. Chop chicken livers into small bits. Mix with soy sauce, sugar, cornstarch, one tablespoon oil and pepper.
2. Heat the remaining oil in a saucepan and saute the ginger and salt for one minute.
3. **Add boiling water and bring back to a boil.**
4. Add roughly chopped spinach and chicken liver mixture. Cover and simmer for about ½ hour.

Serves 6-8.

Corn Egg Flower Soup

¼ lb (125 g) lean pork
4 teaspoons cornstarch
2 tablespoons oil
½ teaspoon sugar
½ teaspoon pepper
2 tablespoons soy sauce
2½ tablespoons water
4 teaspoons salt

2 slices fresh ginger
1 clove garlic
½ onion
1 scallion
6 cups (1½ liters) boiling water
2 cups corn kernels
4 eggs

1. Chop pork finely. Mix with cornstarch, one tablespoon oil, sugar, pepper, soy sauce, 2½ tablespoons water and half the salt.
2. Chop ginger, garlic, onion and scallion (white part only).
3. Heat the remaining oil in a saucepan and saute the ginger, garlic, onion, scallion and remainder of salt for one minute.
4. Add boiling water and corn kernels and bring soup **to a boil**. Reduce heat, cover and simmer for 15 minutes.
5. Add pork mixture, replace cover and simmer for ten minutes.
6. Remove from heat. Beat eggs and gently stir into the soup.

Serves 6-8.

Mixed Vegetable Soup

¼ lb (125 g) mushrooms
4 teaspoons oil
½ lb (250 g) spinach
¼ lb (125 g) green beans

¼ lb (125 g) watercress
6 cups (1½ liters) cold water
2 teaspoons salt
½ teaspoon pepper

1. Cut the mushrooms into thin slices.
2. Heat oil in a saucepan and saute the mushrooms for five minutes.
3. Chop vegetables roughly and add to the mushrooms. Saute for another five minutes.
4. Add water and bring **to a boil**. Reduce heat, cover and simmer for ½ hour.

Serves 6.

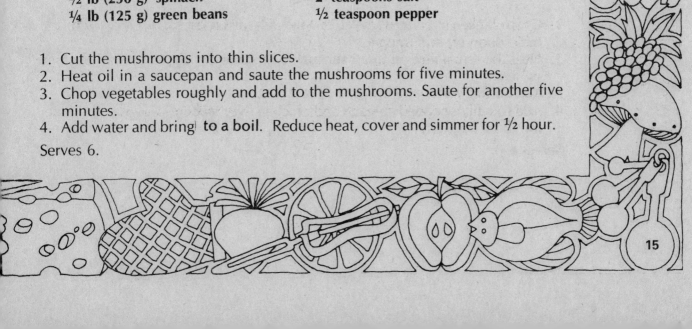

Chicken Noodle Soup

¼ lb (125 g) raw chicken meat
¼ lb (125 g) bamboo shoots
¼ lb (125 g) ham
6 cups (1½ liters) chicken
   stock

1 oz (30 g) egg noodles
salt to taste
2½ tablespoons sherry

1. Cut the chicken into thin slices. Slice the bamboo shoots and ham into strips.
2. Bring the stock to a boil. Add chicken, bamboo shoots and ham and simmer for about ten minutes.
3. Add noodles. Season to taste with salt and simmer for five minutes.
4. Stir in sherry and cook for another five minutes.

Serves 6.

Beef and Watercress Soup

¼ lb (125 g) watercress
½ lb (250 g) lean beef
2 tablespoons soy sauce
2 teaspoons oil

1½ teaspoons salt
6 cups (1½ liters) chicken
   stock
½ teaspoon sesame oil

1. Wash and drain the watercress. Cut off the hard stems.
2. Chop the beef finely. Mix with the soy sauce, oil and salt.
3. In a large saucepan, bring the chicken stock to a boil. Stir in the watercress and return to the boil.
4. Add sesame oil and beef mixture. Stir well. Cover and simmer for about 20 minutes.

Serves 6.

Mushroom Soup

1 clove garlic, sliced
4 teaspoons oil
¼ lb (125 g) fresh mushrooms
1 slice fresh ginger
6 cups (1½ liters) chicken
   stock
salt and sesame oil

1. Saute the garlic in the hot oil for 30 seconds. Remove and discard the garlic.
2. Saute the mushrooms for five minutes.
3. Add ginger and chicken stock and **bring to a boil.** Reduce heat, cover and simmer for one hour.
4. Remove ginger. Add salt to taste and a few drops of sesame oil. Stir well and serve immediately.

Serves 6.

Beef Chowder

¾ cup (155 g) rice
8 cups (2 liters) beef stock
1 oz (30 g) noodles
4 teaspoons oil
2 slices fresh ginger
½ lb (250 g) minced steak

few drops sesame oil
2 teaspoons soy sauce
salt and pepper
2 eggs beaten
scallions, chopped

1. Cook the rice in the beef stock for two hours.
2. Fry the noodles in the oil for a few seconds, then remove.
3. Finely chop the ginger and add with the meat to the rice. Cook for about 15 minutes.
4. Stir in sesame oil, soy sauce and salt and pepper to taste.
5. Put some noodles and a little egg in each soup bowl and pour the chowder over. Garnish with chopped scallions.

Serves 6-8.

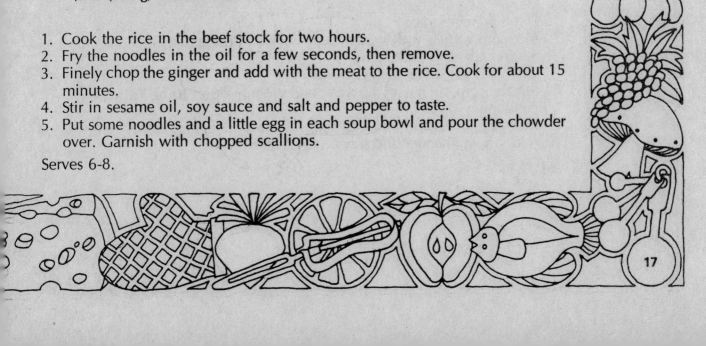

Egg and Scallop Soup

1 lb (500 g) fresh scallops
8 cups (2 liters) chicken stock
1 teaspoon salt
½ teaspoon pepper
3 scallions, chopped
4 eggs, beaten

1. Chop the scallops.
2. Bring chicken stock to the boil in a large saucepan. Add the scallops, salt and pepper and **bring to a boil** again. Reduce heat, cover and simmer for about ½ hour.
3. Stir in the scallions and beaten eggs and serve immediately.

Serves 6-8.

Crab and Corn Soup

½ lb (250 g) crab meat
1½ cups corn kernels
6 cups (1½ liters) chicken stock
2½ tablespoons sherry

2 eggs, separated
2 teaspoons cornstarch
2½ tablespoons water
1 teaspoon salt
½ teaspoon pepper

1. Shred the crab meat
2. Mix corn kernels with the chicken stock and **bring to a boil.**
3. Stir in crab meat and sherry.
4. Gradually stir in beaten egg yolks.
5. Mix the cornstarch with the water and stir into soup. **Bring to a boil,** constantly.
6. Beat egg whites and fold into soup. Cook for a few minutes.
7. Add salt and pepper and serve immediately.

Serves 6.

Bamboo Shoot Soup

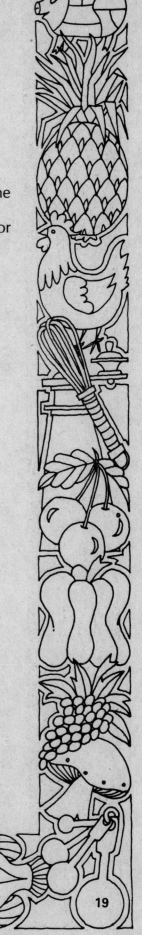

- 1 lb (500 g) bamboo shoots
- 4 teaspoons oil
- 6 cups (1½ liters) chicken stock
- 1 teaspoon salt
- ½ teaspoon pepper
- 4 eggs, beaten
- ½ cup chopped ham
- 4 scallions, chopped

1. Cut the bamboo shoots into strips and saute in oil in a large saucepan for one minute.
2. Pour in chicken stock and bring to a boil. Reduce heat, cover and simmer for ten minutes.
3. Add salt and pepper.
4. Stirring constantly, slowly add the beaten eggs.
5. Add ham and cook for five minutes.
6. Serve immediately, garnished with chopped scallions.

Serves 6.

Sour Soup

⅛ lb (60 g) dried mushrooms
¼ lb (125 g) bamboo shoots
½ lb (250 g) ham, chopped
6 cups (1½ liters) chicken
   stock
2½ tablespoons soy sauce

4 teaspoons vinegar
4 teaspoons cornstarch
5½ tablespoons water
3 eggs, beaten
1½ teaspoons salt
½ teaspoon pepper

1. Soak the mushrooms for ½ hour.
2. Coarsely chop the mushrooms, bamboo shoots and ham.
3. In a large saucepan, bring the chicken stock to a boil. Add the mushrooms, bamboo shoots and ham and simmer for five minutes.
4. Mix together the soy sauce, vinegar, cornstarch and water. Stir into soup and cook for another five minutes.
5. Gradually add the beaten eggs, stirring constantly. Soup should be kept simmering.
6. Add salt and pepper and serve immediately.

Serves 6.

Pork Soup

1½ lbs (750 g) minced pork
2½ tablespoons soy sauce
2 egg yolks
6 cups (1½ liters) water
1 lb (500 g) spinach

1 teaspoon salt
8 whole peppercorns
1 egg plus 2 egg whites,
   beaten

1. Mix together the pork, soy sauce and egg yolks. Form into small balls.
2. Bring water to a boil. Add pork balls and simmer for about 15 minutes.
3. Wash the spinach well and chop roughly. Add to the soup and simmer for five minutes.
4. Add the salt and peppercorns.
5. Slowly add the beaten egg and egg whites, stirring constantly. Serve immediately.

Serves 6-8.

Abalone and Pork Soup

¼ lb (125 g) lean pork
¼ lb (125 g) bamboo shoots
⅛ lb (60 g) dried mushrooms
1 teaspoon cornstarch
4 teaspoons sherry
¼ cup fresh peas

6 cups (1½ liters) chicken stock
2 large slices fresh ginger
3 scallions, chopped
¼ lb (125 g) canned abalone
1 teaspoon salt

1. Slice the pork and bamboo shoots.
2. Soak the mushrooms in water for ½ hour. Drain and chop.
3. Mix the pork, bamboo shoots, mushrooms, cornstarch and sherry.
4. Boil the peas in a little water for three minutes.
5. Bring the chicken stock to a boil and add the peas, ginger, scallions and pork mixture. Simmer for five minutes.
6. Add abalone and salt and simmer for another 5-10 minutes.
7. Remove ginger and serve immediately.

Serves 6-8.

Cabbage and Pork Soup

¼ lb (125 g) lean pork
¼ teaspoon sugar
1 teaspoon salt
2 teaspoons cornstarch
2 teaspoons oil
¾ lb (375 g) cabbage

1 medium carrot
6 cups (1½ liters) water
2 slices fresh ginger
1 teaspoon salt
½ teaspoon sesame oil

1. Cut the pork into thin slices.
2. Blend together the sugar, one teaspoon salt, cornstarch and oil. Marinate the pork in this mixture for about 20 minutes.
3. Chop the cabbage and cut the carrot julienne style.
4. Put the water, ginger and carrot in a saucepan and bring to the boil. Boil for five minutes.
5. Add the cabbage and the pork and return **to a boil**. Reduce heat, cover and simmer for twenty minutes.
6. Stir in one teaspoon salt and sesame oil and serve immediately.

Serves 4.

Lettuce and Fish Soup

½ lb (250 g) fish fillets
2½ tablespoons oil
6 cups (1½ liters) water
2 slices fresh ginger
1½ teaspoons salt
1 lettuce

1. Cut the fish into thin slices.
2. Heat the oil until very hot and quickly saute the fish.
3. Add the water, ginger and salt and bring **to a boil**. Reduce heat and simmer for 15 minutes.
4. Roughly chop the lettuce and add to the soup. Bring **to a boil** and cook only until lettuce is soft.

Serves 4-6.

Steamed Bread

4 teaspoons dried yeast	½ teaspoon salt
3 tablespoons sugar	2 cups flour
½ cup (125 ml) warm water	

1. Mix together the yeast, sugar, salt and flour in a large mixing bowl.
2. Make a well in the center and add the warm water. Mix to a soft dough.
3. Knead on a floured board for ten minutes.
4. Return to the bowl, cover with a damp cloth and put in a warm place to rise for one hour, or until it doubles in size.
5. Knead lightly and again leave to rise until it doubles its size.
6. Roll into a long rope about 1½ inches (4 cm) in diameter. Cut into 1-inch (2½-cm) pieces and roll into ovals 4 inches (10 cm) long.
7. Dust one side with flour and double over. Allow to rise for 15 minutes or until double in size. Cook in a steamer for 10-15 minutes, until light and spongy.

These may be eaten plain or stuffed with sweet or savoury filling. See below.

Sweet Stuffing

2 oz (60 g) walnuts, finely chopped	2 oz (60 g) roasted sesame seeds, crushed
2 oz (60 g) almonds, finely chopped	½ cup sugar
	4 teaspoons lard

Mix all the ingredients together. Use stuffing to fill steamed bread.

Savoury Stuffing

½ lb (250 g) cabbage, finely chopped	¼ teaspoon sugar
¼ lb (125 g) chopped pork meat	1 scallion, finely chopped
1 teaspoon salt	4 teaspoons soy sauce
	1 teaspoon sesame oil

1. Remove as much moisture as possible by squeezing the cabbage in a dry cloth.
2. Combine the cabbage with the other ingredients. Mix well.

23

Rice and Noodles

Special Stirred Rice

2 cups cooked rice
¼ lb (125 g) cooked shrimp
½ cup (125 g) butter or margarine
2 oz (60 g) raisins, chopped
¼ lb (125 g) ham, chopped

6 scallions, chopped
2 oz (60 g) blanched walnuts
2 oz (60 g) blanched almonds
3 tablespoons soy sauce
1 teaspoon salt

1. Re-heat the rice.
2. Shell and de-vein the shrimp. Cut into small pieces.
3. Melt the butter or margarine in a frypan and saute the shrimp for one minute.
4. Add the raisins, ham, scallions, walnuts, almonds, soy sauce and salt. Stir for 2-3 minutes.
5. Add the rice and mix well.

Serves 4-6.

Boiled Rice

1½ tablespoon butter or
    margarine
1 cup rice
1½ cups (375 ml) boiling
    water

1. Melt the butter or margarine in a saucepan.
2. Add the rice and stir over a medium heat until the rice is completely coated.

3. Pour on the boiling water. Stir once or twice and return to a boil. Reduce
   heat, cover and simmer over a low heat for about 20 minutes. Check only
   after 20 minutes. Rice is cooked when all the water is absorbed.

Serves 4.

Steamed Rice

1 cup rice
2½ cups (625 ml) water

1. Wash the rice twice.
2. Put into a saucepan and add the water.
3. **When rice comes to a boil,**   stir and boil for three minutes. Drain.
4. Half fill small rice bowls with the partially cooked rice. Place in the top of a
   large steamer and steam for 1½-2 hours.

Serves 4.

Fried Rice with Shrimp

1 cup rice
½ lb (250 g) shrimp
4 eggs
2 spring onions
3 tablespoons oil
1 teaspoon salt

1. Cook the rice in boiling salted water until tender.
2. Shell and de-vein the shrimp. Cut into small pieces.
3. Chop the onions finely and saute in one tablespoon of oil.
4. Add the shrimp and cook over a high heat for two minutes, stirring constantly. Add the salt and mix well.
5. Beat the eggs and pour over the shrimp. Scramble the mixture but do not allow eggs to set completely. Remove mixture from frypan.
6. Heat the remaining oil in the frypan and saute the drained cooked rice. Stir for about three minutes or until rice is thoroughly heated.
7. Add egg and shrimp mixture and mix well.

Serves 4-6.

Fried Rice with Chicken

3 eggs	¼ lb (125 g) cooked chicken
1 small onion	2 oz (60 g) shrimp
6 mushrooms	⅓ cup (85 ml) oil
¼ cup cooked peas	1 teaspoon salt
1 bamboo shoot	2 cups cooked rice
¼ lb (125 g) ham	3 tablespoons soy sauce

1. Beat eggs and cook in a frypan without stirring. When set, remove from pan and cut into strips. Set aside.
2. Chop the vegetables, ham, chicken and shrimp.
3. Heat two tablespoons oil and the salt in a frypan. Add the rice and saute for about five minutes. Remove from pan and set aside.
4. Heat remaining oil in frypan and saute the onions until golden brown.
5. Add the rest of the vegetables, ham, chicken and shrimp and saute for three minutes.
6. Add the rice and mix well.
7. Add the soy sauce and the egg strips and heat thoroughly. Serve immediately.

Serves 4-6.

Fried Noodles with Vegetables

½ lb (250 g) noodles
¼ lb (125 g) cabbage
¼ lb (125 g) bamboo shoots
¼ lb (125 g) sliced pork
6 fresh mushrooms
4 tablespoons oil
salt

2 tablespoons sherry
3 tablespoons soy sauce
2 slices fresh ginger
¼ lb (125 g) shelled shrimp
4 teaspoons cornstarch
1 teaspoon sesame oil

1. Cook the noodles in boiling salted water until tender. Drain.
2. Cut the cabbage, bamboo shoots and pork into strips.
3. Pour boiling water over the mushrooms and soak for ten minutes. Cut into strips.
4. Heat two tablespoons of the oil in a large frypan. Saute the pork, cabbage, bamboo shoots and mushrooms for four minutes. Season to taste with salt. Remove from heat.
5. Mix together the sherry, soy sauce, ginger, shrimp and cornstarch. Fry in ½ tablespoon oil for two minutes.
6. Remove ginger, stir in the fried pork mixture and fry for another two minutes. Remove the mixture from the frypan and drain.
7. Heat the remaining oil in the frypan and add the drained noodles. Add a little salt and the sesame oil and, stirring constantly, cook for five minutes.
8. Add all the ingredients and stir over a high heat for two minutes.

Serves 6.

Hong Kong Rice

oil
¼ lb (125 g) chopped ham
6 mushrooms, sliced
¼ lb (125 g) diced pork
1 medium onion, chopped
¼ lb (125 g) cooked shrimp

1 green pepper, chopped
1 teaspoon mixed spices
5 cups cooked rice
4 teaspoons soy sauce
salt
pepper

1. Heat a little oil in a frypan and saute the ham, mushrooms, pork, onion, chopped shrimp, pepper and spices. Remove from frypan and keep warm.
2. Add a little more oil to the frypan and saute the rice.
3. Thoroughly mix in the meat and vegetable mixture.
4. Stir in the soy sauce and season to taste with salt and pepper.
5. Stirring constantly, heat for about ten minutes and serve immediately.

Serves 6-8.

Fried Noodles

½ lb (250 g) bean sprouts
½ lb (250 g) lean pork
1 lb (500 g) noodles
oil for frying
2 tablespoons soy sauce

1. Mix together the bean sprouts and sliced meat.
2. Cook the noodles in boiling salted water for seven minutes. Rinse with cold water and drain well.
3. Fry in deep oil for five minutes, until golden brown. Drain.
4. Saute the meat and bean sprouts in one tablespoon oil for five minutes. Mix in the soy sauce and cook for a further two minutes.
5. Serve the noodles with the meat and bean sprouts on the top.

Serves 6.

Fried Noodles with Chicken

½ lb (250 g) cooked chicken meat
3 bamboo shoots
6 mushrooms
½ lb (250 g) egg noodles

oil for frying
1 teaspoon salt
½ teaspoon sesame oil
paprika

1. Cut the chicken meat into small pieces. Slice the bamboo shoots and mushrooms finely.
2. Cook the noodles in boiling salted water until tender. Drain well.
3. Fry the noodles in hot oil in a frypan for two minutes, stirring constantly. Remove and keep warm.
4. Saute the chicken in the oiled pan for about three minutes.
5. Add bamboo shoots, mushrooms, salt and sesame oil. Cook for a further three minutes, stirring occasionally.
6. Pour over the fried noodles and sprinkle with paprika.

Serves 4.

Noodles with Pork and Water Chestnuts

1 lb (500 g) egg noodles	6 mushrooms, chopped
oil for deep frying	1 small onion, chopped
¼ lb (125 g) pork, diced	¼ lb (125 g) bean sprouts
salt and pepper	1 teaspoon cornstarch
2 oz (60 g) water chestnuts,	3 teaspoons soy sauce
shredded	½ teaspoon sesame oil

1. Cook noodles in boiling salted water for five minutes. Rinse with cold water and drain.
2. Heat the oil and deep fry the noodles until golden brown. (Noodles should hold in one piece.) Remove from oil and drain.
3. Saute the pork in a little oil for one minute. Season with salt and pepper.
4. Add the water chestnuts, mushrooms, onion and bean sprouts and cook for two minutes.
5. Blend the cornstarch with the soy sauce and a little water. Add to the pork and water chestnut mixture. Cook for one minute. Stir in the sesame oil.
6. Pour on top of noodles and serve immediately.

Serve 6.

Noodles with Meat

½ lb (250 g) noodles	5 scallions
½ cup (125 ml) oil	¼ lb (125 g) cooked shrimp
½ lb (250 g) lean beef, pork,	2½ tablespoons soy sauce
chicken or ham	salt
4 stalks celery	2 teaspoons cornstarch
6 fresh mushrooms	½ cup (125 ml) water

1. Cook the noodles in boiling salted water for 20 minutes. Rinse with cold water and drain well.
2. Heat two tablespoons of oil over high heat. Fry noodles until slightly brown on one side. Turn and fry on other side. Remove from pan and keep warm.
3. Cut the meat into strips. Slice the celery, mushrooms, scallions and shrimp.
4. Heat the remaining oil, add the meat and shrimp and stir for one minute.
5. Add the vegetables, soy sauce and salt and stir for four minutes.
6. Mix together the cornstarch and water. Add to the mixture, stirring constantly. Cook until sauce is clear.
7. Pour over the noodles and serve immediately.

Serves 4-6.

Noodles with Lobster

½ lb (250 g) noodles
oil for deep frying
¼ lb (125 g) cooked lobster
   meat
¼ lb (125 g) mushrooms

1 onion, sliced
2 bamboo shoots, sliced
1 teaspoon salt
pepper
1 teaspoon cornstarch

1. Boil the noodles in boiling salted water for ten minutes. Rinse with cold water. Drain.
2. Heat one inch (2½ cm) deep of oil in a 8-inch (20-cm) frypan. Add noodles and cook gently for a few minutes. Remove from frypan (noodles should hold together) and drain. Keep warm.
3. Pour off most of the oil from frypan. Saute the lobster and vegetables for one minute. Season and cook for five minutes, stirring occasionally.
4. Add a little water to the cornstarch and stir into the lobster mixture. Cook until smooth and clear. Pour over the noodles and serve immediately.

Serves 4-6.

Rice with Pork and Corn

2 cups hot cooked rice
½ lb (250 g) minced pork
1 teaspoon cornstarch
1 teaspoon oil
3 teaspoons soy sauce
pinch of pepper
1 egg
2 spring onions

2 cloves garlic, crushed
oil for frying
1 teaspoon salt
½ lb (250 g) canned creamed
   corn
¾ cup (185 ml) water
2 teaspoons cornstarch
2½ tablespoons water

1. Marinate the minced pork in a mixture of the cornstarch, oil, soy sauce and pepper for 15 minutes.
2. Beat the egg and chop the spring onions finely.
3. Heat a little oil and saute the garlic and pork for three minutes. Stir in salt.
4. Add the corn and water, cover and cook for five minutes.
5. Mix together cornstarch and 2½ tablespoons of water and add to the pork mixture.
6. Mix in the egg and the spring onions. Cook for three minutes.
7. Pour the pork mixture over the rice and serve immediately.

Serves 2-3.

Rice with Chicken Sauce

2 cups hot cooked rice	1 slice fresh ginger, crushed
1 chicken breast	oil for frying
4 teaspoons sherry	2 teaspoons cornstarch
4 teaspoons soy sauce	¾ cup (185 ml) water
½ teaspoon sugar	1 teaspoon salt
pinch pepper	1 egg, beaten
1 teaspoon cornstarch	1 spring onion, finely
1 egg white	chopped

1. Remove the chicken meat from the bone and dice. Marinate in a mixture of the sherry, soy sauce, sugar, pepper, cornstarch and egg white.
2. Heat 2 tablespoons of oil and saute the ginger for one minute. Add the chicken and cook until the meat turns white.
3. Mix together the cornstarch, water and salt and add to the chicken. Cook until the cornflour is clear. Stir in the egg and remove from heat.
4. Pour the chicken sauce over the rice and serve immediately. Garnish with chopped spring onion.

Serves 2-3.

Congee

1 cup (210 g) rice
1 teaspoon salt
4 teaspoons oil
10 cups (2½ liters) water
1 teaspoon salt

1. Wash the rice thoroughly. Drain.
2. Mix the rice with the salt and oil and set aside for 15 minutes.
3. Bring the water to a boil and add the rice. Return to the boil, then reduce the heat and simmer for 1½ hours. Add second teaspoon salt and mix well.

Serves 6.

Vegetable Fried Rice

2 cups (420 g) rice
6 dried mushrooms (soaked, liquid reserved)
2 leeks
3 stalks celery
½ lb (250 g) bean sprouts
½ lb (250 g) green beans
2 medium carrots, grated
1 cup sliced bamboo shoots

4 tablespoons oil
2 teaspoons sesame oil
1½ teaspoons grated ginger
2 cloves garlic, crushed
1 cup chopped scallions
½ cup (125 ml) mushroom liquid
2½ tablespoons soy sauce

1. Cook the rice, drain and dry thoroughly.
2. Cut the drained mushrooms into thin slices.
3. Wash and slice the leeks and celery. String the beans and cut into thin slices.
4. Heat the oils in a large frypan and saute the ginger and garlic for one minute.
5. Add mushrooms, leeks, celery, bean sprouts, green beans, carrots and bamboo shoots. Stir constantly over a high heat for three minutes.
6. Add rice, mix well and cook until thoroughly heated.
7. Add scallions, mushroom liquid and soy sauce and stir until well mixed. Add salt to taste.

Serves 6.

Stirred Rice

¼ lb (125 g) ham
2 oz (60 g) blanched almonds
2½ tablespoons oil
¼ lb (125 g) peeled shrimp

3 scallions, chopped
3 tablespoons soy sauce
1 teaspoon salt
2 cups cooked rice

1. Cut the ham and almonds into shreds.
2. Heat the oil in a frypan and saute the de-veined shrimp for two minutes.
3. Add the ham, almonds and scallions and stir for one minute.
4. Add the soy sauce, salt and rice and stir for about two minutes.

Serves 4-6.

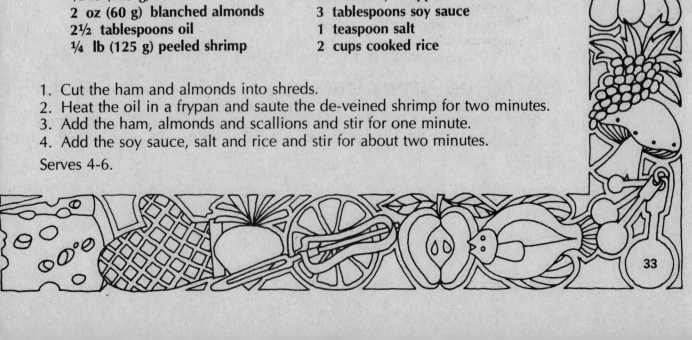

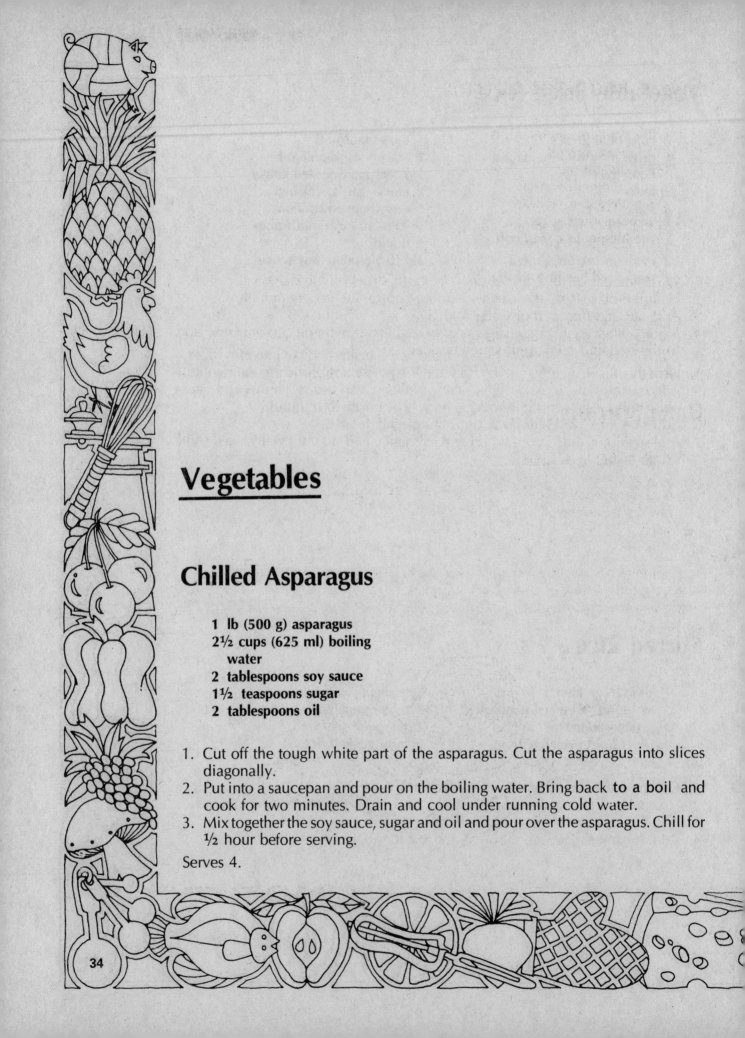

Vegetables

Chilled Asparagus

1 lb (500 g) asparagus
2½ cups (625 ml) boiling
   water
2 tablespoons soy sauce
1½ teaspoons sugar
2 tablespoons oil

1. Cut off the tough white part of the asparagus. Cut the asparagus into slices diagonally.
2. Put into a saucepan and pour on the boiling water. Bring back **to a boil** and cook for two minutes. Drain and cool under running cold water.
3. Mix together the soy sauce, sugar and oil and pour over the asparagus. Chill for ½ hour before serving.

Serves 4.

Sweet and Sour Carrots

1 lb (500 g) medium carrots
2½ tablespoons oil
1½ teaspoons salt
2 cups (500 ml) water
2½ tablespoons vinegar
2½ tablespoons sugar
2½ tablespoons cornstarch

1. Wash the carrots but do not peel. Cut into slices on the diagonal.
2. Heat the oil and fry the carrots, stirring constantly, for one minute.
3. Add salt and one cup of water and boil for five minutes.
4. Mix together the vinegar, sugar; cornstarch and remaining cup of water. Add to the pan and cook until sauce is clear.

Serves 4-6.

Bean Sprouts

1 lb (500 g) bean sprouts
4 teaspoons oil
4 teaspoons soy sauce
few drops sesame oil
salt

1. Fry the bean sprouts in the oil over a medium heat for one minute.
2. Mix in the soy sauce, sesame oil and salt to taste. Cover, reduce heat and cook for five minutes. Remove cover and cook for another 2-3 minutes.

Serves 4.

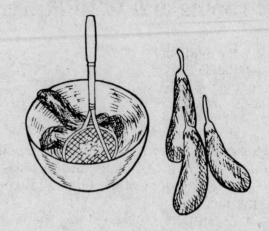

Eggplant

4 small eggplants
½ cup (125 ml) oil
2 cloves garlic, crushed
3 tablespoons soy sauce
1 teaspoon salt

1. Cut the eggplants into ½ inch (1 cm) slices.
2. Heat the oil and fry the eggplant for one minute on each side.
3. Add the garlic, soy sauce, salt and 1¼ cups (300 ml) water.
4. Bring to a boil. Reduce heat, cover and simmer for about 15 minutes.

Serves 4-6.

Fried Scallion Cakes

4 cups flour
1¼ cups (300 ml) water
½ lb (250 g) scallion, chopped
   finely
lard for frying

Filling:
4 tablespoons scallions,
   chopped
4 teaspoons lard
1 teaspoon salt

1. Mix together the flour, water and scallions. Add more water if necessary to form a soft dough.
2. Divide into six equal parts. Roll out each portion very thinly in an oblong shape.
3. Mix together the ingredients for the filling and spread on each of the six portions. Roll up and coil round to form a flat cake. Roll very lightly with a rolling pin to about 6 inches (15 cm) in diameter.
4. Melt the lard and fry the cakes for two minutes on each side over a medium heat. Reduce the heat and fry for a further three minutes on each side or until golden brown on the outside and soft on the inside.

Serves 6.

Mushrooms and Cauliflower

1 small cauliflower	1 cup (250 ml) chicken stock
3 tablespoons oil	1½ tablespoons sherry
¼ lb (125 g) mushrooms	2½ tablespoons soy sauce
6 water chestnuts	2½ tablespoons cornstarch

1. Cut the cauliflower into flowerets. Pour boiling water over them and allow to stand for five minutes. Drain and set aside.
2. Heat two tablespoons of the oil in a saucepan and saute the mushrooms for one minute.
3. Add the chestnuts, chicken stock, sherry, soy sauce, cornstarch and the remaining oil.
4. **Bring to a boil**. Reduce heat and simmer for one minute, stirring constantly.
5. Add the cauliflower and cook for another minute, mixing well.

Serves 4-6.

Fried Celery

1 lb (500 g) celery, sliced	1 teaspoon salt
2½ tablespoons oil	1 small carrot, chopped
2 cloves garlic, crushed	4 teaspoons sherry
1 teaspoon grated ginger	½ teaspoon sesame oil

1. Put celery in boiling water for one minute. Drain well.
2. Heat the oil in a large frypan and saute the garlic and the ginger for 30 seconds.
3. Add the salt, carrot and drained celery. Cook for 3 minutes, stirring constantly.
4. Stir in the sherry and sesame oil and serve immediately.

Serves 4.

Celery

  1 bunch celery
  4 teaspoons oil
  1 teaspoon salt

1. Wash celery well. Drain and dry.
2. Cut in thin slices.
3. Heat oil and toss celery in it for one minute.
4. Add salt and cook for another two minutes, stirring constantly.

Serves 4-6.

Celery with Mushrooms

  1   bunch of celery
  2½   tablespoons oil
  ¼   lb (125 g) mushrooms
  2½   tablespoons soy sauce
  4   teaspoons salt
  1   teaspoon sugar

1. Wash, drain and dry the celery. Cut into one-inch (2½-cm) pieces.
2. Heat the oil in a frypan and saute the mushrooms for one minute.
3. Stir in the soy sauce, salt and sugar.
4. Add celery and saute for about three minutes.

Serves 4-6.

Sweet and Sour Radishes

50 small radishes
1½ teaspoons salt
4 teaspoons soy sauce
4 teaspoons vinegar
2½ tablespoons sugar
2 teaspoons oil

1. Wash, drain and dry the radishes. Trim both ends.
2. Partly crush each radish but ensure that they remain whole. Sprinkle on the salt, mix well and allow to stand for ten minutes.
3. Mix together the soy sauce, vinegar, sugar and oil.
4. Toss the radishes in the dressing. Serve cold.

Serves 6.

Fresh Mushrooms

1 lb (500 g) fresh mushrooms
2½ tablespoons oil
2 tablespoons soy sauce
1 teaspoon salt
½ teaspoon sugar
2½ tablespoons cornstarch

1. Slice the mushrooms and saute in hot oil for three minutes.
2. Add soy sauce and fry for another two minutes.
3. Mix together salt, sugar, cornstarch and a little water.
4. Add to the mushrooms and cook until the sauce is clear.

Serves 4-6.

Mixed Vegetables

1 carrot	oil for frying
¼ lb (125 g) bamboo shoots	1 cup cooked peas
½ lb (250 g) cabbage	1 teaspoon salt
¼ lb (125 g) fresh buttton mushrooms	1 teaspoon sugar
2 teaspoons lemon juice	¾ cup (375 ml) water
2 slices fresh ginger	4 teaspoons water
	1 teaspoon cornstarch

1. Slice the carrot, bamboo shoots and cabbage.
2. Cut the mushrooms in halves and sprinkle with the lemon juice.
3. Heat a little oil and saute the ginger for ½ minute. Add the bamboo shoots and carrot and saute for another minute.
4. Add the cabbage and peas and mix well.
5. Mix together the salt, sugar and water and stir into the vegetable mixture. Cover and cook for ten minutes.
6. Add the mushrooms and cook for another five minutes.
7. Mix the 4 teaspoons of water with the teaspoon of cornstarch and add to the vegetables. Cook until clear.

Serves 2.

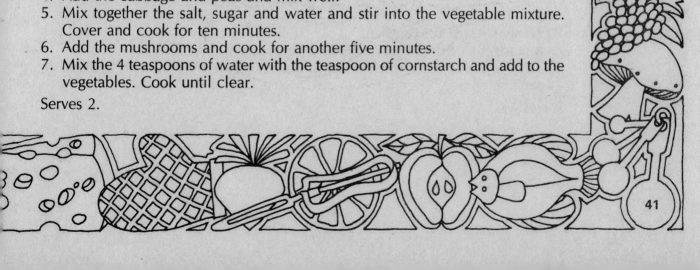

Chop Suey

4 tablespoons oil
1 stalk celery, sliced
1 onion, sliced
2 oz (60 g) bean sprouts
3 small tomatoes, skinned
   and sliced
¼ lb (125 g) mushrooms,
   sliced
½ lb (250 g) sliced cooked
   chicken

1½ cups (375 ml) chicken
   stock
1 teaspoon salt
¼ teaspoon pepper
4 teaspoons soy sauce
4 teaspoons cornstarch
5½ tablespoons water

1. Heat oil. Add vegetables and saute for five minutes.
2. Mix in chicken, stock, salt and pepper and cook for another five minutes.
3. Add soy sauce and mix well.
4. Blend cornstarch with water and stir into the chicken mixture. Cook until thick and serve immediately.

Serves 6.

Cold Cucumbers

2 large cucumbers, peeled
1½ teaspoons salt
3 tablespoons soy sauce
2½ tablespoons vinegar
2 teaspoons sugar
4 teaspoons oil

1. Thinly slice the cucumbers.
2. Mix together the salt, soy sauce, vinegar, sugar and oil.
3. Toss the cucumbers in the dressing and allow to stand for about ½ hour before serving.

Serves 4-6.

Braised Vegetables

2 lb (1 kg) mixed vegetables (cabbage, leeks, beans, cauliflower, scallions, snow peas)
4 tablespoons oil
1 teaspoon sesame oil
2 cloves garlic, crushed

1½ teaspoons grated ginger
½ cup (125 ml) hot water
4 teaspoons soy sauce
½ teaspoon salt
1 tablespoon cornstarch
4 teaspoons water

1. Saute the garlic and ginger in the hot oils for one minute.
2. Add the vegetables and cook for two minutes, stirring constantly.
3. Add hot water, soy sauce and salt, mix well, cover and cook for 5 minutes over a low heat.
4. Mix together the cornstarch and water and stir into vegetables. Cook for three minutes. Serve immediately.

Serves 6.

Stuffed Peppers

4 green peppers
1 large bamboo shoot
¾ lb (375 g) minced pork
4 teaspoons soy sauce
1½ teaspoons cornstarch
salt

1. Cut the pepper in half and remove the seeds.
2. Chop the bamboo shoot and mix with the pork.
3. Add the soy sauce, cornstarch and salt to taste to the pork mixture.
4. Fill the peppers and steam for about 45 minutes.

Serves 4 or 8.

Spinach and Shrimp

2 lb (1 kg) spinach
3 oz (90 g) dried shrimp
1½ teaspoons salt
2½ tablespoons oil
3 tablespoons soy sauce

1. Wash the spinach very well. Put the spinach without any additional water into a large saucepan, cover and cook for about five minutes. Drain and chop.
2. Put the shrimp in a saucepan with 1½ cups (375 ml) water and bring to a boil. Remove from heat and let stand for ½ hour. Remove shrimp but reserve the water. Chop the shrimp.
3. Mix together all ingredients including the shrimp water. Serve cold.

Serves 4-6.

Braised Mushrooms and Bamboo Shoots

¼ lb (125 g) dried mushrooms
   (soaked, liquid reserved)
2 lb (1 kg) canned bamboo
   shoots
4 slices fresh ginger
oil for frying
3 cups (750 ml) mushroom
   liquid

2 teaspoons salt
1 teaspoon sugar
4 tablespoons water
1 teaspoon sesame oil
4 teaspoons cornstarch

1. Cut the bamboo shoots into thick slices.
2. Heat a little oil and saute the ginger until brown.
3. Add the mushroom and bamboo shoots and cook for one minute.
4. Stir in the mushroom liquid, salt and sugar. Cover and cook over a medium heat for 30-45 minutes.
5. Mix together the water, sesame oil and cornstarch and stir into the mushroom mixture. Cook until cornflour is clear.

Serves 4.

Mushrooms in White Sauce

oil for frying
1 lb (500 g) small mushrooms
1 cup (250 ml) chicken stock
2 cups (500 ml) milk
2½ tablespoons cornstarch

2 teaspoons salt
1 teaspoon sesame oil
¼ teaspoon pepper
4 tablespoons chopped ham

1. Heat a little oil and saute the mushrooms for two minutes.
2. Stir in the stock and cook for another two minutes. Remove from heat and set aside.
3. Mix together a little of the milk and the cornstarch, then slowly add the remainder of the milk, the salt, sesame oil and pepper. Cook, stirring constantly until it thickens.
4. Pour over the mushrooms and sprinkle the chopped ham over the top.

Serves 4-6.

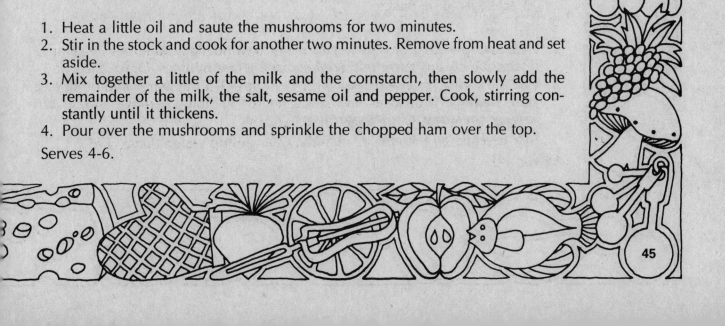

Spinach with Minced Pork

1 lb (500 g) spinach	½ teaspoon salt
¼ lb (125 g) minced pork	¼ teaspoon sugar
1 teaspoon soy sauce	1 clove garlic, crushed
¼ teaspoon sugar	1 cup (250 ml) water
1 teaspoon cornstarch	¼ teaspoon sesame oil
oil for frying	1 teaspoon cornstarch

1. Wash, drain and dry the spinach and chop coarsely.
2. Mix together the pork, soy sauce, sugar and cornstarch. Allow to stand for ten minutes.
3. Heat a little oil and saute the spinach with the salt and sugar for one minute. Cover and cook for five minutes. Remove spinach and keep warm.
4. Heat a little more oil and saute the garlic for one minute. Add the pork and saute until the pork is cooked.
5. Mix together the water, sesame oil and cornstarch and add to the pork mixture. Cook until the cornstarch is clear. Pour over the spinach and serve immediately.

Serves 3-4.

Baked Vegetables

1 lb (500 g) Chinese cabbage
1 lb (500 g) cauliflower
¾ teaspoon baking soda
1 lb (500 g) button mushrooms
oil for frying
1 lb (500 g) fresh asparagus,
   cooked

½ cup flour
4 cups (1 liter) stock
¾ cup (185 ml) milk
1½ tablespoons butter
¼ lb (125 g) chopped ham

1. Cut the cabbage into strips and the cauliflower into flowerets.
2. Put about one cup of water in a saucepan, add the baking soda and bring to a boil. Add the cabbage and cook for five minutes. Strain and set aside.
3. In the same water, cook the cauliflower for ten minutes. Strain and set aside.
4. Heat a little oil in a frypan and saute the mushrooms for two minutes. Set aside.
5. Put the cooked asparagus on the bottom of a buttered baking dish. Arrange the other vegetables on top.
6. Mix together the flour and a little of the stock in a saucepan. Gradually add the remainder of the stock and the milk. Cook until it becomes light and creamy. Add the butter and stir until the butter melts. Pour over the vegetables and sprinkle the ham on the top.
7. Bake in a 350°F (180°C) oven for ½ hour.

Serves 4.

Marrow in Cream Sauce

1 vegetable marrow (500 g -1 lb)	½ cup (125 ml) milk
¼ lb (125 g) mushrooms	2 teaspoons cornstarch
oil for frying	½ teaspoon sesame oil
	1 teaspoon salt

1. Peel and seed the marrow and cut into pieces about 2 inches by 4 inches (5 cm by 10 cm). Cook in boiling salted water until tender. Strain and set aside.
2. Slice the mushrooms and saute in a little hot oil for two minutes.
3. Mix together the milk, cornstarch, sesame oil and salt. Stir into the mushrooms and cook until light and creamy.
4. Pour over the marrow and serve immediately.

Serves 4.

Fried Bean Sprouts

3 scallions, sliced	1 lb (500 g) bean sprouts
1 teaspoon grated ginger	¼ lb (125 g) diced ham
2½ tablespoons oil	1 teaspoon sesame oil
1 teaspoon salt	

1. Saute the scallions and ginger in the hot oil for two minutes.
2. Add the salt and bean sprouts and cook for five minutes.
3. Add the ham and the sesame oil and mix well. Cook until the ham is heated through.

Serves 4.

Stuffed Peppers

½ lb (250 g) lean pork
3 teaspoons oil
½ teaspoon sugar
2 teaspoons soy sauce
1 teaspoon salt
2 teaspoons cornstarch
pinch pepper
1 teaspoon water
2½ tablespoons dried shrimp
   (soaked and chopped)
1 oz (30 g) dried mushrooms
   (soaked, liquid reserved)

6 medium green peppers
flour
oil for frying
1 teaspoon salt
½ cup (125 ml) mushroom
   liquid
1 teaspoon cornstarch
1 teaspoon soy sauce
¼ teaspoon sesame oil

1. Chop the pork very finely and marinate it in a mixture of the oil, sugar, soy sauce, salt, cornstarch, pepper and water. Add the shrimp and mushrooms, mix well and allow to stand for ten minutes.
2. Cut the peppers into halves lengthwise and remove the core and seeds. Sprinkle a little flour on the inside of each half. Fill each half with the meat mixture. Press filling down firmly.
3. Fry the peppers in a little hot oil, meat side down. Sprinkle salt over the peppers. Cover and cook over a medium heat for five minutes. Turn over and cook on the other side for five minutes. Remove from pan and keep warm.
4. Mix together the mushroom, liquid, cornstarch, soy sauce and sesame oil. Cook in the same pan until smooth, stirring constantly. Pour over the peppers and serve immediately.

Serves 6.

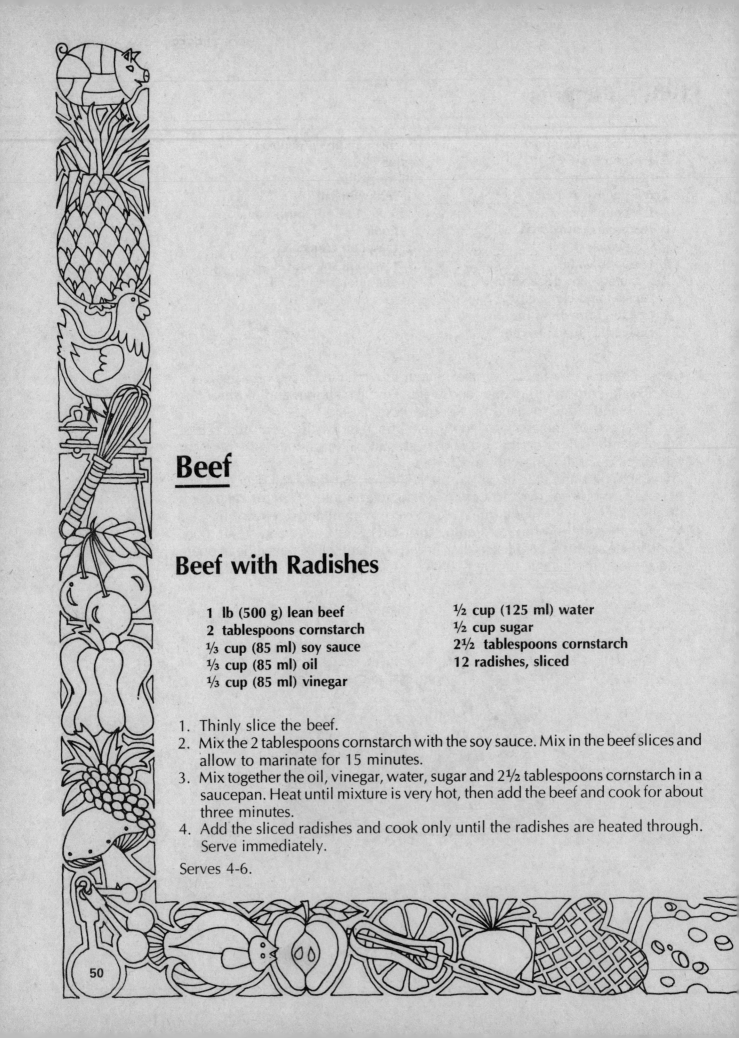

Beef

Beef with Radishes

1 lb (500 g) lean beef
2 tablespoons cornstarch
⅓ cup (85 ml) soy sauce
⅓ cup (85 ml) oil
⅓ cup (85 ml) vinegar

½ cup (125 ml) water
½ cup sugar
2½ tablespoons cornstarch
12 radishes, sliced

1. Thinly slice the beef.
2. Mix the 2 tablespoons cornstarch with the soy sauce. Mix in the beef slices and allow to marinate for 15 minutes.
3. Mix together the oil, vinegar, water, sugar and 2½ tablespoons cornstarch in a saucepan. Heat until mixture is very hot, then add the beef and cook for about three minutes.
4. Add the sliced radishes and cook only until the radishes are heated through. Serve immediately.

Serves 4-6.

Fried Kidney

1 lb (500 g) kidney	½ lb (250 g) celery
2½ tablespoons cornstarch	3 scallions
2 teaspoons sherry	oil for frying
2 slices fresh ginger, chopped	4 teaspoons soy sauce

1. Cut kidney into small slices.
2. Mix together the cornstarch, sherry and ginger and add to the sliced kidney.
3. Slice the celery and scallions into fine strips and saute for about two minutes in a tablespoon of oil.
4. Add the kidney and another tablespoon of oil and fry over a high heat for five minutes.
5. Stir in the soy sauce, cook for another 30 seconds and serve immediately.

Serves 4.

Beef and Broccoli

1 lb (500 g) lean beef	½ lb (250 g) broccoli
1 clove garlic, crushed	2 teaspoons cornstarch
1 teaspoon salt	2 tablespoons water
1 teaspoon grated ginger	2 tablespoons soy sauce
2 teaspoons cornstarch	4 tablespoons oil
½ teaspoon five-spice powder	1½ teaspoons sesame oil

1. Cut the beef into very thin slices.
2. Mix together the salt, garlic and ginger. Combine with the beef slices.
3. Toss the beef in the cornstarch mixed with the five-spice powder.
4. Cut the broccoli into small sprigs.
5. Mix the cornstarch, water and soy sauce.
6. Heat both oils in a frypan and saute the beef for about two minutes.
7. Add the broccoli and cook for five minutes, stirring constantly.
8. Stir in the cornstarch mixture, mix well and cook until thick. Serve immediately.

Serves 4-6.

Beef with Green Peppers

1 lb (500 g) lean beef
¼ cup (65 ml) oil
1 teaspoon salt
pepper
1 scallions, cut up
1 clove garlic, crushed
3 green peppers, sliced

3 stalks celery, sliced
1¼ cups (300 ml) chicken
    stock
2 teaspoons cornstarch
½ cup (125 ml) water
2 teaspoons soy sauce

1. Cut the beef into thin slices. Heat the oil until very hot, add the seasonings and saute the beef for one minute, stirring constantly.
2. Add the scallion, garlic, green peppers and celery. Cook for one minute.
3. Add the chicken stock, cover and simmer for ten minutes.
4. Mix together the cornstarch, water and soy sauce. Add to the beef, mix well and cook until thick. Serve immediately.

Serves 4.

Chinese Tripe

1 lb (500 g) cooked tripe
2½ tablespoons sesame oil
2 medium onions, chopped
1 clove garlic, crushed
2½ tablespoons sherry

½ cup (125 ml) water
2 tablespoons soy sauce
5 fresh mushrooms
2 medium tomatoes

1. Slice the tripe into thin strips.
2. Heat the oil and lightly fry the tripe with the onions and garlic.
3. Stir in the sherry, water, soy sauce, sliced mushrooms and tomatoes.
4. Gently simmer for ½ hour.

Serves 4.

Beef Lo Mein

½ lb (250 g) egg noodles
1 lb (500 g) lean beef
4 teaspoons oil
4 teaspoons soy sauce
pinch pepper
1 onion, finely chopped
oil for frying

2 cloves garlic, crushed
2 teaspoons salt
1 cup (250 ml) water
4 teaspoons sherry
1 teaspoon sugar
2 teaspoons soy sauce
4 teaspoons cornstarch

1. Boil the noodles in salted water until tender. Strain and set aside.
2. Chop the beef finely.
3. Mix together the oil, soy sauce and pepper. Marinate the beef in this mixture for ten minutes.
4. Saute the onion and garlic in a little hot oil for two minutes. Add the beef and cook for another two minutes or until beef is almost cooked. Add salt and mix well.
5. Mix together the water, sherry, sugar, soy sauce and cornstarch and add to the beef mixture. Cook until cornstarch is clear.
6. Add the noodles and mix well. Serve immediately.

Serves 4.

Beef and Bean Sprouts

1 lb (500 g) lean beef
1 egg white
1 teaspoon salt
4 teaspoons soy sauce
¼ teaspoon sugar

2½ tablespoons sherry
4 teaspoons cornstarch
2 teaspoons oil
2½ tablespoons water
1 lb (500 g) bean sprouts

1. Cut the beef into very thin slices.
2. Mix together the egg white, salt, soy sauce, sugar and sherry. Add the beef and marinate for ½ hour.
3. Heat a little oil in a frypan and saute the beef mixture for two minutes.
4. Mix together the cornstarch, oil and water and add to the beef mixture. Cook until the cornstarch is clear. Set aside.
5. Saute the bean sprouts in a little hot oil for two minutes. Mix with the beef and serve immediately.

Serves 4-6.

Beef Chop Suey

½ lb (250 g) lean beef
2 teaspoons oil
2 teaspoons soy sauce
1 teaspoon sugar
1 teaspoon salt
4 teaspoons cornstarch
¼ teaspoon pepper
2 small onions
2 carrots
oil for frying

½ cabbage
3 slices fresh ginger, crushed
1 teaspoon sugar
2 teaspoons salt
4 cloves garlic, crushed
1 cup (250 ml) water
4 teaspoons cornstarch
2 teaspoons soy sauce
1 teaspoon sugar

1. Cut the beef into thin slices and marinate in a mixture of the oil, soy sauce, sugar, salt, cornstarch and pepper for ten minutes.
2. Finely chop the onions, carrots and cabbage.
3. Heat a little oil and saute the onions until transparent. Set aside.
4. Saute the carrots for one minute. Set aside.
5. Saute the ginger for one minute, add cabbage and cook another minute.
6. Add the onions and carrots, mix well and add the one teaspoon sugar and 2 teaspoons salt. Remove and set aside.
7. Heat a little oil and saute the garlic. Add the beef and cook for two minutes.
8. Mix together the water, cornstarch, soy sauce and sugar and stir into the beef. Cook until cornstarch is clear and pour beef mixture over the vegetables.

Serves 4.

Fried Liver

1 lb (500 g) liver
1 tablespoon cornstarch
3 tablespoons sherry
4 slices fresh ginger
1 onion

6 fresh mushrooms
½ lb (250 g) bamboo shoots
sesame oil for frying
4 teaspoons soy sauce

1. Cut the liver into small pieces. Mix with the cornstarch, sherry and ginger.
2. Slice the onion, mushrooms and bamboo shoots.
3. Heat a little oil in a frypan and fry the liver and vegetables over a high heat, stirring constantly. Cook until golden, not more than eight minutes.
4. Add soy sauce and mix thoroughly. Serve immediately.

Serves 4-6.

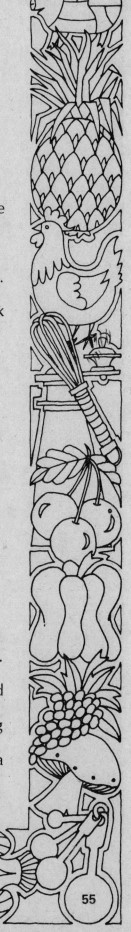

Braised Beef and Noodles

½ lb (250 g) egg noodles	2½ tablespoons oil
1 lb (500 g) lean beef	½ cup (125 ml) soy sauce
1 clove garlic, crushed	½ cup (125 ml) water
1 teaspoon salt	2 teaspoons cornstarch
½ teaspoon grated ginger	4 teaspoons water
¼ teaspoon five-spice powder	6 scallions sliced

1. Cook the noodles in boiling salted water until just tender. Drain and rinse under cold water.
2. Cut the beef into very thin slices.
3. Mix together the garlic, salt, ginger, and five-spice powder. Mix with the beef.
4. Heat the oil in a frypan and saute the beef over a high heat for two minutes.
5. Mix together the soy sauce and water. Add to the beef and bring to a boil.
6. Mix together the cornstarch and 4 teaspoons water. Stir into the beet and cook until smooth and thick.
7. Add noodles, mix well and heat thoroughly.
8. Add the scallions and stir for another minute. Serve immediately.

Serves 4-6.

Quick Fried Beef with Peppers

1 lb (500 g) lean beef	2½ tablespoons sherry
1 red pepper	1 clove garlic, crushed
2 green peppers	1 slice fresh ginger
1 teaspoon salt	3 scallions, sliced
4 teaspoons soy sauce	6 tablespoons oil
¼ teaspoon pepper	2½ tablespoons beef stock

1. Cut the beef into thin slices.
2. Remove the seeds from the peppers and cut them into ½-inch (one-cm) slices.
3. Mix together the salt, soy sauce, pepper, sherry, garlic, ginger and scallions. Add the beef and allow to marinate at room temperature for ½ hour.
4. Heat half the oil and saute the peppers for one minute. Remove from pan and set aside.
5. Heat the remaining oil and add the beef. Cook for about two minutes, stirring constantly.
6. Return the peppers to the pan and mix well. Add the stock and cook over a high heat for one minute.

Serves 4.

Beef Chow Mein

½ lb (250 g) fine egg noodles	1 teaspoon salt
1 lb (500 g) lean beef	oil for frying
2 teaspoons water	1 teaspoon salt
4 teaspoons soy sauce	2 teaspoons salt
1 teaspoon baking soda	1 cup (250 ml) water
4 teaspoons oil	4 teaspoons soy sauce
2 teaspoons sherry	1 teaspoon sesame oil
pinch pepper	4 teaspoons cornstarch
2 eggs	2 cloves garlic, crushed
½ medium cabbage	2½ tablespoons sesame seeds

1. Cook the noodles in boiling salted water for one minute, stirring constantly. Drain and rinse under cold water. Allow to cool.
2. Cut the beef into thin strips.
3. Mix together the water, soy sauce, baking soda, oil, sherry and pepper. Add the beef and allow to marinate for 15 minutes.
4. Beat the eggs with one teaspoon salt and cook like an omelette. Remove from pan and cut into strips.
5. Shred the cabbage. Saute the cabbage with the one teaspoon salt for one minute, stirring constantly. Remove from pan and set aside.
6. Heat three tablespoons of oil in a frypan and fry the noodles, stirring frequently. Add the two teaspoons of salt. Cook until the noodles are golden brown. Remove from pan and drain on absorbent paper.
7. Mix together the water, soy sauce, sesame oil and cornstarch.
8. Heat a little oil in a frypan and saute the garlic and the beef until the beef is almost cooked. Add the cabbage and mix well.
9. Add the cornstarch mixture and cook until the cornstarch is clear.
10. Pour the beef mixture over the noodles. Garnish with the egg strips and the roasted sesame seeds.

Serves 4.

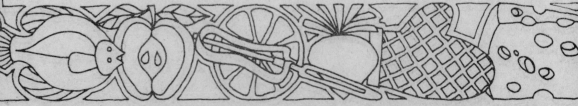

Beef and Long Beans

1 lb (500 g) long beans	2 teaspoons cornstarch
1 lb (500 g) lean beef	2½ tablespoons water
1 clove garlic, crushed	2½ tablespoons oyster sauce
1 teaspoon grated ginger	2 tablespoons soy sauce
1 teaspoon salt	2½ tablespoons oil
½ teaspoon five-spice powder	½ cup (125 ml) beef stock

1. Cut beans into one-inch (2½-cm) lengths.
2. Cut beef into very fine slices. Mix with the garlic, ginger, salt and five-spice powder.
3. Blend the cornstarch with the water, oyster sauce and soy sauce.
4. Heat the oil in a frypan and saute the beef and beans over a high heat for 2-3 minutes. Add stock and bring to a boil.
5. Stir in the cornstarch mixture and cook until the sauce thickens. Serve immediately.

Serves 4-6.

Chicken

Chicken with Almonds

1 lb (500 g) chicken	2 teaspoons salt
1/3 cup (85 ml) oil	2 teaspoons cornstarch
1/4 lb (125 g) blanched almonds	2 teaspoons sugar
	4 teaspoons soy sauce
1/4 lb (125 g) mushrooms	3 teaspoons sherry
1 green pepper	1 1/4 cups (300 ml) water
2 bamboo shoots	boiled rice
1 onion	

1. Cut the chicken into cubes.
2. Heat one tablespoon of the oil in a frypan. Saute the almonds until golden brown. Remove from the oil.
3. Chop the mushrooms, pepper, bamboo shoots and onion.
4. Heat another two tablespoons of the oil in the frypan and saute the onion for two minutes.
5. Add the chicken cubes and fry until the chicken is slightly brown.
6. Add the mushrooms, pepper and bamboo shoots along with one teaspoon of salt and the rest of the oil and cook for about five minutes, stirring constantly.
7. In a small saucepan blend together the remaining salt, the cornstarch, sugar, soy sauce, sherry and water. Bring to a boil, stirring constantly. Pour over the chicken, add the almonds and cook until very hot. Serve immediately with the boiled rice.

Serves 4.

Egg Fu Yong

½ lb (250 g) cooked chicken
½ lb (250 g) onions
3 spring onions
¼ lb (125 g) mushrooms
¼ lb (125 g) bamboo shoots
½ lb (250 g) tomatoes,
   blanched and skinned

oil for frying
salt and pepper
chicken stock
4 teaspoons soy sauce
4 teaspoons cornstarch
2½ tablespoons water
2 eggs, well-beaten

1. Cut the chicken into small pieces. Slice the vegetables thinly.
2. Saute the vegetables in a little oil for five minutes. Add the chicken and cook for another three minutes.
3. Season to taste with salt and pepper. Pour on enough chicken stock to cover, add the soy sauce and cook for three minutes.
4. Mix the cornstarch with the water. Add to vegetable and chicken mixture and cook until thickened.
5. In a small frypan make an omelette with the eggs.
6. Put the chicken and vegetables on a serving platter and place the omelette on top. Serve immediately. Serves 4.

Chicken Balls with Lychees

Chicken Balls:
½ lb (250 g) cooked chicken
½ onion, chopped
6 water chestnuts
6 medium mushrooms
4 teaspoons cornstarch
salt
4 teaspoons soy sauce
1 teaspoon sherry

1 egg white, stiffly beaten
oil for deep frying

Sauce:
1 can lychees in syrup
½ cup (125 ml) chicken
   stock
4 teaspoons soy sauce
4 teaspoons cornstarch
1 scallion

1. To make the chicken balls, finely chop the chicken and the vegetables. Mix together with the cornstarch, salt, soy sauce, sherry and stiffly beaten egg white. Shape into small balls and fry in deep oil until golden brown. Drain.
2. To make the sauce, mix ½ cup of lychee syrup and the chicken stock and bring to a boil. Mix the soy sauce and the cornstarch and add to the lychee mixture. Cut the scallion into 1-inch (2½-cm) pieces and add along with the drained lychees and the chicken balls to the sauce. Heat thoroughly and serve immediately. Serves 4.

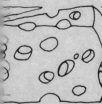

Chicken Lo Mien

¼ lb (125 g) fine egg noodles	1¼ cups (300 ml) chicken stock
¼ lb (125 g) cooked chicken	2½ tablespoons cornstarch
2 stalks celery	4 tablespoons water
6 mushrooms	2½ tablespoons soy sauce
1 cup bean sprouts	salt and pepper
2½ tablespoons oil	

1. Cook the noodles in boiling salted water for ten minutes. Rinse in cold water and drain.
2. Cut chicken and vegetables into shreds.
3. Saute the chicken in the hot oil for two minutes. Add vegetables and saute for another two minutes.
4. Add stock and mix well. Cover, reduce heat and simmer for ten minutes.
5. Mix together cornstarch, water and soy sauce and add to the chicken and vegetable mixture. Season to taste with salt and pepper.
6. Stir in the noodles, re-heat and serve immediately.

Serves 4-6.

Fried Sliced Chicken

1 lb (500 g) raw white chicken meat	
¼ lb (125 g) green beans	1 clove garlic
½ green pepper	2 teaspoons oil
¼ lb (125 g) mushrooms	salt and pepper
1 medium onion	4 teaspoons sherry
	½ teaspoon sugar

1. Slice the chicken thinly and coat each piece with oil. Set aside.
2. Cut up beans and boil for two minutes in salted water. Drain.
3. Slice the mushrooms and the onion.
4. Saute the whole garlic in the oil for one minute. Remove the garlic and saute the onion. Season to taste with salt and pepper. When the onion is transparent, remove and keep warm.
5. In the same frypan, cook the chicken until tender.
6. Add vegetables, sherry and sugar, mix well and heat thoroughly before serving.

Serves 4.

Chicken with Mushrooms

3 lb (1½ kg) chicken
2 tablespoons soy sauce
12 dried mushrooms, soaked
2 medium bamboo shoots
4 water chestnuts
oil for deep frying
6 slices fresh ginger
1½ teaspoons salt

2½ cups (625 ml) water
½ teaspoon sugar
¼ teaspoon pepper
2 scallions, cut into 1-inch
  (2½-cm) pieces
3 teaspoons cornstarch
4 tablespoons water

1. Cut the chicken in half and rub inside and out with soy sauce.
2. Slice the mushrooms, bamboo shoots and water chestnuts into shreds.
3. Heat about 1 inch (2½ cm) of oil in a frypan and when it is very hot, fry the chicken on each side for about three minutes. Remove and drain.
4. In the same frypan saute the ginger and the salt for one minute. Add the mushrooms, bamboo shoots, water chestnuts, water, sugar, pepper and scallions. Mix well.
5. Add the chicken, cover and cook over a low heat for 20 minutes.
6. Remove the chicken and chop into small pieces. Put on a serving dish.
7. Mix the cornstarch with the water and stir into the vegetable mixture. Cook until clear and thick. Pour over the chicken and serve immediately.

Serves 4.

Chicken with Walnuts

½ lb (250 g) white chicken
  meat
1 teaspoon cornstarch
2 tablespoons soy sauce
½ teaspoon salt

¼ teaspoon pepper
¼ teaspoon sugar
4 teaspoons oil
4½ oz (120 g) walnuts
¼ lb (125 g) smoked ham

1. Cut the chicken into thin slices.
2. Blend together the cornstarch, 1 teaspoon soy sauce, ¼ teaspoon each of salt, pepper, sugar and oil.
3. Blanch the walnuts in boiling water and then fry in hot oil for one minute. Drain on absorbent paper and sprinkle with remaining ¼ teaspoon salt.
4. Heat a little oil in a frypan and saute the chicken for one minute.
5. Chop ham and add to the chicken with the walnuts.
6. Sprinkle with the remaining soy sauce and cook until chicken is tender.
7. Stir in the cornstarch mixture and heat through.

Serves 2-4.

Chicken with Green Peppers

4 chicken breasts
1 teaspoon salt
pinch of pepper
1½ teaspoons soy sauce
1½ teaspoons cornstarch
1 egg white, slightly beaten
2 large green peppers
oil for frying

1 clove garlic, crushed
½ teaspoon fresh ginger,
  crushed
1 red chilli, finely chopped
4 teaspoons sherry
2 teaspoons soy sauce
¼ teaspoon sugar

1. Remove the chicken meat from the bone and cut into small cubes.
2. Mix together the salt, pepper, soy sauce and cornstarch. Mix in the chicken pieces. Allow to stand for ten minutes. Add the slightly beaten egg whites and mix well.
3. Remove the seeds from the peppers and cut into small squares. Heat a little oil and saute the peppers for one minute. Remove from the oil and set aside.
4. Saute the garlic in a little hot oil for about one minute. Add the chicken and cook for a further minute, stirring constantly.
5. Add the peppers and saute for another five minutes.
6. Stir in the ginger, chilli, sherry, soy sauce and sugar and cook for two minutes.

Serves 4.

Chicken with Ginger and Onions

4 chicken breasts
8 spring onions
oil for frying
3 teaspoons crushed ginger
1 teaspoon salt

4 teaspoons sherry
2½ tablespoons soy sauce
½ teaspoon sugar
½ teaspoon sesame oil

1. Remove the chicken meat from the bones and cut into cubes.
2. Chop the onions.
3. Heat oil in large frypan. Saute the onion, ginger and salt for one minute.
4. Add the chicken and mix well. Cook for two minutes.
5. Add the sherry, soy sauce, sugar and sesame oil. Cover and cook for 5-10 minutes or until chicken is tender.

Serves 4.

Lemon Chicken

1 chicken (1½ kg - 3 lb)
juice of ½ lemon
2 teaspoons sugar
1 teaspoon soy sauce
4 teaspoons sherry
2 teaspoons soy sauce
3 slices fresh ginger

¾ cup (185 ml) water
2 teaspoons sugar
1½ teaspoons salt
1 small lemon, sliced
1½ teaspoons cornstarch
½ teaspoon sesame oil
3 teaspoons water

1. Mix together the lemon juice, 2 teaspoons sugar, one teaspoon soy sauce and the sherry. Rub the inside of the chicken with this mixture.
2. Rub the outside of the chicken with the two teaspoons of soy sauce. Allow to stand for about ½ hour at room temperature.
3. Saute the ginger in a little oil for two minutes.
4. Add the chicken and brown on all sides.
5. Mix the ¾ cup water with the leftover marinade and add to the chicken.
6. Stir in the second two teaspoons of sugar and the salt. Add the lemon slices.
7. Cover and cook over a medium heat for 20 minutes, turning occasionally.
8. Remove chicken from pan and cut into one-inch (2½-cm) pieces. Keep warm.
9. Mix together the cornstarch, sesame oil and the three teaspoons of water. Pour into the pan and when it thickens, pour over the chicken. Serves 4-6.

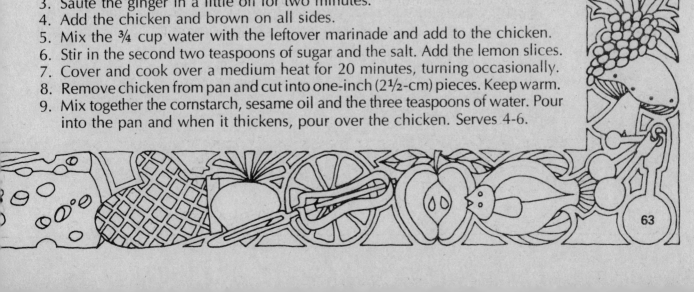

Chicken with Honey

1 chicken (1½ kg - 3 lb)	oil for frying
1 tablespoon soy sauce	4 tablespoons honey
3 spring onions, chopped	4 teaspoons soy sauce
3 slices fresh ginger, crushed	2 tablespoons water
1½ teaspoons salt	

1. Rub the outside of the chicken with the one tablespoon of soy sauce.
2. Mix together the onions, ginger and salt and rub the inside of the chicken with this mixture.
3. Heat some oil in a frypan and brown the chicken, turning frequently.
4. Mix together the honey, soy sauce and water and add to the frypan.
5. Bring to a boil. Reduce heat and cook over a very low heat for about two hours. Turn chicken occasionally. Add a little water when necessary.

Serves 4.

Chicken with Celery

4 chicken breasts	
½ teaspoon salt	½ teaspoon salt
1½ tablespoon sherry	1 slice fresh ginger, crushed
4 stalks celery	4 tablespoons water
1 egg white	2 teaspoons cornstarch
2 teaspoons cornstarch	1 teaspoon soy sauce
oil	½ teaspoon sesame oil

1. Remove the chicken meat from the bone and cut into thin slices.
2. Mix together the salt and sherry and marinate the chicken slices in it for ½ hour.
3. Cut the celery into thin strips lengthwise—about 1½ inches (4 cm) in length.
4. Mix the chicken with the egg white and 2 teaspoons of cornstarch.
5. Saute the celery in a little oil for two minutes. Add ½ teaspoon salt and set aside.
6. Saute the ginger in a little oil, then add the chicken and cook until the chicken is tender.
7. Add the celery, mix well and cook for two minutes.
8. Blend together the water, 2 teaspoons cornstarch, soy sauce and sesame oil. Stir into the chicken mixture and cook until the cornstarch is clear.

Serves 4.

Chicken with Pineapple

2 large chicken breasts
3 slices canned pineapple
⅓ cup (85 ml) oil
½ cup sliced Chinese cabbage
3 stalks celery, sliced
8 water chestnuts

½ cup sliced bamboo shoots
2 teaspoons salt
1 teaspoon sugar
pepper
4 teaspoons cornstarch
4 tablespoons cold water

1. Put the chicken in a saucepan and cover with water. Boil for 15-20 minutes. Remove from the water and cool. When cool, slice meat into 1-inch (2½-cm) squares.
2. Cut the pineapple into chunks.
3. Saute the pineapple and the vegetables in the oil for two minutes.
4. Add the chicken, salt, sugar and pepper to taste. Pour in 4 cups (1 liter) of water and stir well. Cover and cook for about five minutes over a medium heat.
5. Mix the cornstarch with the cold water and stir into the chicken and pineapple mixture. Cook until the sauce is thick. Serve immediately.

Serves 4.

Deep Fried Chicken Livers

1½ lb (750 g) chicken livers
4 tablespoons soy sauce
4 tablespoons sherry
4 tablespoons vinegar
½ teaspoon salt

¼ teaspoon pepper
½ cup flour
1¼ teaspoons baking powder
oil for deep frying

1. Cut the chicken livers into bite-size pieces.
2. Mix together the soy sauce, sherry, vinegar, salt and pepper and marinate the chicken livers in this mixture for ½ hour.
3. Blend together the flour, baking powder and enough water to make a thick batter.
4. Coat the chicken livers in the batter and deep fry in hot oil.
5. Drain on absorbent paper and serve immediately.

Serves 6.

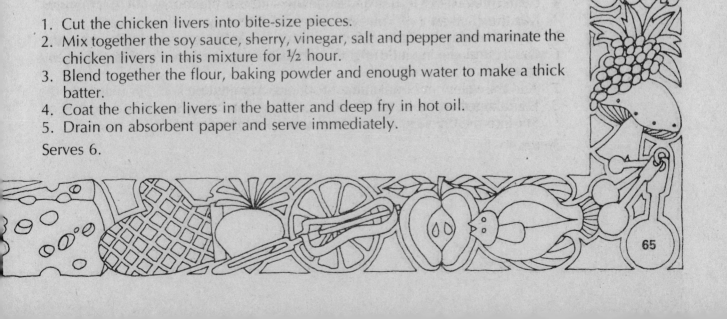

Chicken with Coconut

4 chicken breasts
1½ teaspoons salt
1½ teaspoons cornstarch
pinch of pepper
½ cup desiccated coconut
1½ cups (375 ml) hot water
oil for frying

½ teaspoon salt
3 teaspoons cornstarch
⅓ cup (85 ml) milk
2 egg whites
1½ tablespoons desiccated
coconut

1. Remove the chicken meat from the bone and cut into thin slices. Do not discard the chicken bones.
2. Mix together the salt, cornstarch and pepper and toss the chicken slices in this mixture.
3. Soak the ½ cup coconut in the hot water for ½ hour in a saucepan. Add the **chicken bones and bring to a boil. Reduce heat and simmer for 20 minutes. Strain.**
4. Heat a little oil in a frypan and saute the chicken slices for about four minutes. Remove from pan and put into a baking dish.
5. Mix the strained coconut liquid with the ½ teaspoon salt, 3 teaspoons corn-starch and the milk. Bring to a boil stirring constantly. Pour over the chicken in the baking dish.
6. Beat the egg whites until stiff and spread over the chicken. Sprinkle with the 1½ tablespoons coconut.
7. Bake in a 450°F (230°C) oven for about ten minutes.

Serves 4.

Chicken and Nuts

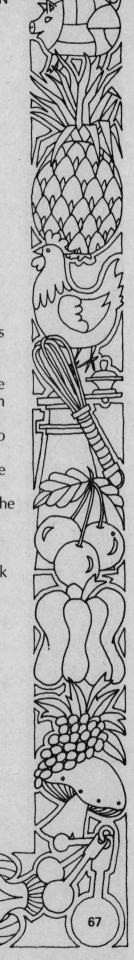

4 chicken breasts
1 teaspoon salt
1½ teaspoons soy sauce
3 teaspoons cornstarch
¼ teaspoon pepper
2 egg whites, slightly beaten
oil for frying
½ cup unsalted peanuts
½ cup walnuts
½ cup cashews
½ cup almonds

1 teaspoon salt
1 oz (30 g) dried
   mushrooms, soaked
1 teaspoon sugar
2½ tablespoons mushroom
   liquid
¼ cup (65 ml) mushroom
   liquid
2 teaspoons soy sauce
2 teaspoons cornstarch

1. Remove the meat from the bones and cut the chicken into small cubes.
2. Mix together the teaspoon of salt, soy sauce, cornstarch and pepper and toss the chicken in this mixture. Allow to stand for ten minutes.
3. Mix the chicken into the egg whites.
4. Put enough oil in a frypan to cover the bottom of the pan to a depth of one inch (2½ cm). Heat until very hot. Remove from heat and fry the chicken cubes for ½ minute. Drain and keep warm.
5. Saute the peanuts, walnuts, cashews and almonds in the hot oil for about two minutes. Drain and sprinkle with one teaspoon salt. Set aside.
6. Drain the soaking mushrooms (reserving the liquid) and chop. Saute the mushrooms for one minute. Pour off all but a little of the oil.
7. Add the sugar and the 2½ tablespoons of the mushroom liquid to the mushrooms. Cover and cook for one minute.
8. Add the chicken, mix well and cook for three minutes.
9. Add the nuts and mix well.
10. Stir in the ¼ cup of mushroom liquid, the soy sauce and cornstarch and cook until the cornflour is clear.

Serves 4.

Chicken and Cashews

4 chicken breasts
1½ tablespoons sherry
1 teaspoon sesame oil
2 teaspoons soy sauce
2 teaspoons oil
pinch of pepper
1 teaspoon sugar
4 teaspoons cornstarch
2 oz (60 g) dried mushrooms
   (soaked and liquid reserved)
½ cup canned bamboo shoots

oil for frying
½ lb (250 g) cashew nuts
2 tablespoons water
1 cup fresh peas, cooked
2 teaspoons salt
1 cup (250 ml) mushroom
   liquid
4 teaspoons cornstarch
1 teaspoon sugar
2 teaspoons soy sauce

1. Remove the chicken meat from the bone and dice.
2. Mix together the sherry, sesame oil, soy sauce, oil, pepper, sugar and cornstarch. Add the chicken and marinate for 20 minutes.
3. Dice the mushrooms and bamboo shoots.
4. Heat a little oil and saute the cashew nuts until brown. Remove from frypan and set aside.
5. Saute the mushrooms in a little hot oil for a minute then add the 2 tablespoons of water and cook for another minute. Remove from frypan and set aside.
6. Saute the bamboo shoots and peas for about two minutes. Remove from frypan and set aside.
7. Saute the chicken in a little hot oil until just cooked. Add cashews, mushrooms, bamboo shoots and peas. Add the salt.
8. Mix ½ cup of mushroom liquid with cornstarch, sugar and soy sauce and add to the chicken mixture. Cook until the cornstarch is clear.

Serves 4.

Chicken Curry

1 chicken (1½ kg - 3 lb)
4 teaspoons cornstarch
1½ teaspoons salt
1 lb (500 g) potatoes
½ lb (250 g) onions
oil for frying
3 slices fresh ginger, crushed
5 cloves garlic, crushed

4 teaspoons curry powder
1½ cups (375 ml) water
1½ teaspoons salt
1½ tablespoons sherry
¾ cup desiccated coconut
1 cup (250 ml) unsweetened condensed milk

1. Cut the chicken into 1½-inch (4-cm) cubes.
2. Mix together the cornstarch and salt and toss the chicken cubes in this mixture.
3. Peel and cut the potatoes into 1½-inch (4-cm) cubes.
4. Peel and cut the onions into 1½-inch (4-cm) pieces.
5. Heat a little oil and saute the chicken for about five minutes, stirring occasionally. Remove from pan and set aside.
6. Saute the ginger, garlic and onions for ½ minute, then add the curry powder, mix well and cook for another ½ minute.
7. Add the chicken and potatoes and mix thoroughly.
8. **Mix together the water, salt and sherry and add to the chicken. Bring to a** boil. Reduce heat, cover and simmer for ten minutes.
9. Put coconut in a colander and place over boiling water. Cover and steam for 20 minutes.
10. Remove chicken, potatoes and onions from saucepan and place in a casserole dish.
11. Mix the coconut and milk with the curry sauce and pour over the chicken. Cover and bake in a 350°F (180°C) oven for ½ hour.

Serves 4.

Chicken Chow Mein

½ lb (250 g) fine egg noodles
4 chicken breasts
2 teaspoons soy sauce
pinch pepper
pinch sugar
2 egg whites
2 onions
oil for frying

1 teaspoon salt
2 cloves garlic, crushed
1 cup (250 ml) water
4 teaspoons cornstarch
1 teaspoon salt
2 teaspoons soy sauce
½ teaspoon sesame oil

1. Cook the noodles in boiling salted water for one minute, stirring to separate. Strain, rinse under cold running water and let cool.
2. Remove the chicken meat from the bone and cut into thin slices.
3. Mix together the soy sauce, pepper, sugar and egg whites. Stir into the chicken slices and allow to marinate for 15 minutes.
4. Cut the onions into thin strips.
5. Heat ½ cup (125 ml) oil in a frypan. When the oil is very hot, add the noodles. Cook the noodles for a few minutes on each side. (The noodles will form into a firm cake.) Remove from pan and set aside.
6. Saute the onion and the garlic for one minute.
7. Add the chicken and saute for two minutes.
8. Mix together the water, cornstarch, salt, soy sauce and sesame oil. Add to the chicken and cook until the cornstarch is clear. Pour over the noodles and serve immediately.

Serves 4.

Braised Chicken Livers

1 lb (500 g) chicken livers
1 scallion
2 slices fresh ginger
⅓ cup (85 ml) soy sauce
4 teaspoons sugar
1½ tablespoons sherry
2 cups (500 ml) water

CONTINUED ON NEXT PAGE

1. Wash and trim the chicken livers and cut in halves.
2. Put the livers in boiling water. Bring back to a boil. Remove and drain.
3. Cut the scallion into three pieces. Lightly pound the ginger slices.
4. Mix together the soy sauce, sugar, sherry and water.
5. Put chicken livers in a heavy saucepan with the scallion, ginger and soy sauce mixture. Braise over medium heat until almost all the liquid is gone.

Serves 4.

Chicken in Soy Sauce

1 chicken (1½ kg - 3 lb)	2 slices fresh ginger, crushed
1½ tablespoons sherry	2 cloves garlic, crushed
1½ tablespoons soy sauce	4 tablespoons soy sauce
2 teaspoons salt	¾ cup (185 ml) water
¼ teaspoon pepper	4 teaspoons sugar
oil for frying	

1. Mix together the sherry, soy sauce, salt and pepper and rub the inside and the outside of the chicken with this mixture. Allow to stand at room temperature for about one hour.
2. Heat a tablespoon of oil in a large saucepan and saute the ginger and garlic for about one minute. Add the soy sauce and bring to the boil.
3. Pour this mixture into the chicken and put the chicken into the saucepan. When the sauce drains out, pour it back in. Repeat this a few times.
4. Turn the chicken in the sauce to completely coat the outside. Then bring sauce to the boil. Roll the chicken over occasionally to brown on all sides.
5. Add the water and the sugar and cook over a medium heat for 20 minutes or until chicken is cooked. Turn chicken a few times during cooking. Add a little more water if necessary.
6. Cut the chicken into bite-size pieces and pour the sauce over it.

Serves 4.

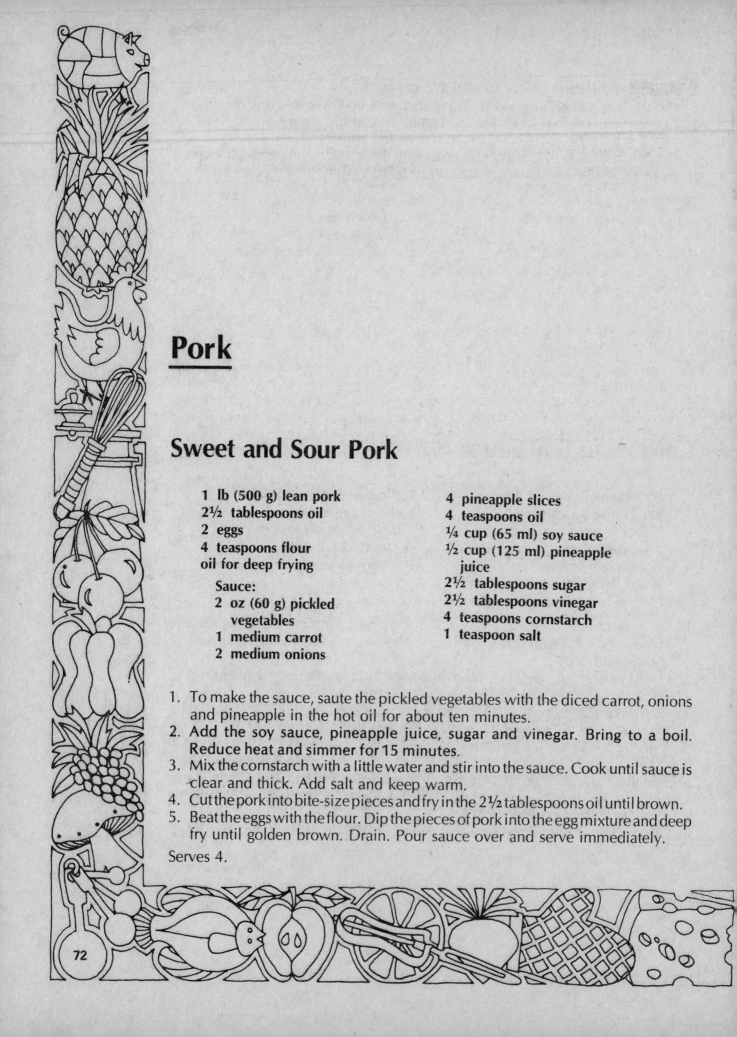

Pork

Sweet and Sour Pork

1 lb (500 g) lean pork
2½ tablespoons oil
2 eggs
4 teaspoons flour
oil for deep frying

Sauce:
2 oz (60 g) pickled
    vegetables
1 medium carrot
2 medium onions

4 pineapple slices
4 teaspoons oil
¼ cup (65 ml) soy sauce
½ cup (125 ml) pineapple
    juice
2½ tablespoons sugar
2½ tablespoons vinegar
4 teaspoons cornstarch
1 teaspoon salt

1. To make the sauce, saute the pickled vegetables with the diced carrot, onions and pineapple in the hot oil for about ten minutes.
2. Add the soy sauce, pineapple juice, sugar and vinegar. Bring to a boil. Reduce heat and simmer for 15 minutes.
3. Mix the cornstarch with a little water and stir into the sauce. Cook until sauce is clear and thick. Add salt and keep warm.
4. Cut the pork into bite-size pieces and fry in the 2½ tablespoons oil until brown.
5. Beat the eggs with the flour. Dip the pieces of pork into the egg mixture and deep fry until golden brown. Drain. Pour sauce over and serve immediately.

Serves 4.

Spring Rolls

won ton wrappers
5 dried mushrooms (soaked, liquid reserved)
¼ lb (125 g) lean pork
¼ teaspoon sugar
1 teaspoon cornstarch
½ teaspoon salt
pinch pepper
2 teaspoons soy sauce
1 teaspoon water

3 cups bean sprouts
1 teaspoon salt
4 teaspoons mushroom liquid
1 clove garlic, crushed
1 teaspoon cornstarch
¼ teaspoon sugar
2½ tablespoons mushroom liquid
1 egg, beaten

1. Cut the mushrooms into very thin slices.
2. Cut the pork into thin slices.
3. Mix together the sugar, cornstarch, salt, pepper, soy sauce and water and add the pork to this mixture. Marinate the pork in this mixture for ten minutes.
4. Saute the mushrooms in a little oil for one minute, add the bean sprouts and cook for a further two minutes. Stir in the salt and 1½ tablespoons mushroom liquid. Cover and cook for a few minutes. Set aside.
5. Saute the garlic and the pork for two minutes. Add the mushroom and bean sprout mixture and mix well.
6. Mix together the cornstarch, sugar and 2½ tablespoons mushroom liquid and add to the pork mixture. Cook until it thickens.
7. Put about 1-2 tablespoons of the filling in each won ton wrapper (depending on the size of the wrapper). Brush the beaten egg on the edges and roll up lengthwise. Fold in both ends and again seal the joins with egg. Deep fry until golden brown.

Makes 12-15.

Sweet and Sour Pork with Pineapple and Peppers

1 egg
½ cup flour
1 teaspoon salt
1 lb (500 g) lean pork
oil for deep frying
1½ cups pineapple chunks

1 green pepper
½ cup (125 ml) vinegar
2½ tablespoons brown sugar
1½ tablespoons molasses
2½ tablespoons cornstarch

1. Mix together the egg, flour, salt and enough water (about 5 tablespoons) to make a batter.
2. Cut the pork into bite-size pieces and dip into the batter.
3. Heat the oil and when hot, deep fry the pork pieces until brown. Remove and drain on absorbent paper.
4. In a saucepan combine the pineapple chunks, green pepper, vinegar, sugar, molasses and about ½ cup water. Bring to a boil, stirring constantly.
5. Mix the cornstarch with ½ cup water and add to the sauce. Stir until it thickens then add the meat and heat thoroughly. Serve immediately.

Serves 4-6.

Pork with Walnuts

1 lb (500 g) lean pork
2½ tablespoons soy sauce
3 teaspoons brown sugar
2½ tablespoons flour
1 cup (250 ml) oil for frying
3 oz (90 g) shelled walnuts

1. Cut the meat into thin slices.
2. Mix one tablespoon of the soy sauce, the sugar and flour. Coat the pork with this mixture.
3. Heat most of the oil in a frypan. Cook the pork in the hot oil until it is crispy and brown. Drain.
4. In a separate frypan, heat a little oil and saute the walnuts for about three minutes.
5. Add the pork and stir in the remaining soy sauce. Cook for another three minutes and serve immediately.

Serves 4.

Pork with Peanuts and Peppers

2½ tablespoons oil
2½ tablespoons soy sauce
1 lb (500 g) lean pork, diced
3 carrots, diced
¼ lb (125 g) peanuts
3 green peppers, sliced
2½ tablespoons brown sugar

1. Heat the oil until very hot. Remove from heat and stir in the soy sauce.
2. Add pork to soy sauce mixture and let stand for five minutes.
3. Return to heat and cook with the carrots for three minutes.
4. Add peanuts and pepper and cook for about five minutes.
5. Add the brown sugar, mix well and serve immediately.

Serves 4.

Sweet and Sour Pork Spareribs

2 lb (1 kg) pork spare ribs
1 cup (250 ml) soy sauce
1 cup (250 ml) pineapple juice
½ cup (125 ml) sherry
2½ tablespoons brown sugar
1 clove garlic, crushed

1. Cut the pork between the bones.
2. Mix together the soy sauce, pineapple juice, sherry, brown sugar and garlic.
3. Marinate the spare ribs in this mixture for several hours.
4. Cook under a hot broiler for about seven minutes on each side.

Serves 4-6.

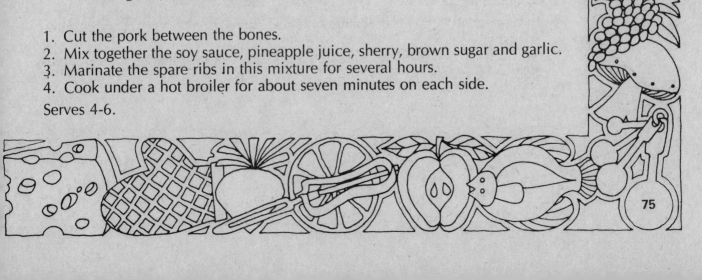

Pork and Cucumber

    1 lb (500 g) lean pork
    4 teaspoons cornstarch
    2 teaspoons salt
    ½ cup (125 ml) olive oil
    1 cucumber, chopped
    1¼ cups (300 ml) chicken
       stock
    4 spring onions

1. Mix the pork with the cornstarch, salt and four tablespoons of the oil. Marinate for 20 minutes.
2. Heat the remaining oil in a frypan and saute the pork mixture until it is golden brown.
3. Stir in the cucumber and stock. Bring to a boil. Reduce heat, cover and simmer for abour five minutes.
4. Add the finely chopped onions and continue to cook for two minutes.

Serves 4.

Spareribs with Black Beans

    3 lb (1½ kg) spareribs, cut into   1 teaspoon vinegar
       small pieces   2½ tablespoons soy sauce
    4 tablespoons black beans   ½ cup (125 ml) chicken stock
    2 cloves garlic, crushed   4 tablespoons sherry
    2 teaspoons grated ginger   ½ cup (125 ml) oil
    1 teaspoon sugar   2 medium onions, sliced

1. Soak the black beans in water for ½ hour.
2. Combine the black beans with the garlic and ginger.
3. Mix together the sugar, vinegar, soy sauce, chicken stock and sherry. Add to the black bean mixture.
4. Heat the oil in a frypan and saute the spareribs for about 5 minutes.
5. Add the black bean and soy sauce mixture. Mix well and cook for one minute.
6. Add the onions, cover and cook for about 20 minutes.

Serves 6.

Pork with Peanuts

½ cup peanuts
oil for deep frying
1 lb (500 g) lean pork
1 egg white
2 teaspoons cornstarch
¼ teaspoon salt
2 dried red peppers, seeded
  and sliced
2 cloves garlic, crushed
6 scallions, chopped

2 green peppers, chopped
2½ tablespoons sherry
2 teaspoons cornstarch
4 teaspoons water
4 teaspoons soybean paste
2½ tablespoons soy sauce
3 teaspoons sugar
1 teaspoon vinegar
½ teaspoon salt

1. Deep fry the peanuts in hot oil until golden brown. Remove and drain on absorbent paper.
2. Cut pork into cubes and coat with a mixture of egg white, cornstarch and salt. Deep fry the pork until just cooked. Remove and set aside.
3. Saute the garlic and red pepper in a little hot oil for one minute. Add scallions and green peppers and continue cooking for another minute.
4. Add pork and sherry.
5. Mix together the cornstarch and water.
6. Combine the soybean paste, soy sauce, sugar, vinegar and salt. Stir into the pork.
7. Add the cornstarch mixture and cook until thick.
8. Mix in the peanuts, heat through and serve immediately.

Serves 4.

Fried Pork and Vegetables

½ lb (250 g) lean pork
1 egg
2 teaspoons soy sauce
2 teaspoons sherry
¼ teaspoon pepper
oil for frying
1 green pepper, sliced
2 bamboo shoots, sliced
1 leek, sliced

1 stalk celery, sliced
cayenne pepper to taste

Sauce:
2½ tablespoons vinegar
¼ cup sugar
4 teaspoons tomato sauce
4 teaspoons cornstarch

1. Cut the pork into bite-size pieces.
2. Mix all the sauce ingredients together with enough water to make a thin mixture.
3. Beat the egg and mix with the soy sauce, sherry and pepper.
4. Dip the pork pieces into the sauce, then into the egg mixture. Fry in hot oil for about two minutes. Drain.
5. Fry all the vegetables in the same oil for two minutes. Add the meat and cayenne pepper, mix well and cook for another minute.
6. Add the remaining sauce and cook over a high heat for 30 seconds. Add more sherry if desired.

Serves 4.

Fish and Seafood

Fried Fish in Sweet and Sour Sauce

1 lb (500 g) fish fillets
2 eggs
¼ cup cornstarch
oil for deep frying
3 tomatoes, skinned
2½ tablespoons sweet pickles
4 teaspoons oil

⅔ cup (165 ml) water
2½ tablespoons vinegar
2½ tablespoons sugar
3 teaspoons molasses
2½ tablespoons soy sauce
4 teaspoons cornstarch
2½ tablespoons water

1. Cut the fish into 1-inch (2½-cm) cubes.
2. Beat eggs slightly and add to the cornstarch. Mix until smooth.
3. Dip each cube of fish into the batter and fry in deep fat until golden brown. Drain.
4. Saute the tomatoes and pickles in the oil for about ten minutes.
5. Stir in the water, vinegar, sugar, molasses and soy sauce and cook for fifteen minutes.
6. Mix the cornstarch with the water and stir into the tomato and pickle mixture. Pour over the fish and serve immediately.

Serves 4.

Fish with Vegetables

¼ lb (125 g) bamboo shoots	fish stock
½ cucumber	1 lb (500 g) fish fillets
¼ lb (125 g) button mushrooms	flour
salt and pepper	4 teaspoons soy sauce
4 teaspoons oil	2 teaspoons cornstarch

1. Cut the vegetables into small pieces, season with salt and pepper and saute in the oil for two minutes.
2. Add enough stock to cover and simmer for about five minutes.
3. Toss the fish in the flour and fry in an oiled frypan until golden brown.
4. Add soy sauce and cornstarch mixed with a little water to the vegetables. Cook for one minute. Pour over the fish and serve immediately.

Serves 3-4.

Steamed Fish Sliced

1 lb (500 g) fish fillets	1½ tablespoons vinegar
1 teaspoon salt	1½ tablespoons sherry
3 scallions, chopped	1 teaspoon sugar
2 slices fresh ginger, chopped	¼ lb (125 g) sliced ham
2 tablespoons soy sauce	6 large mushrooms, sliced

1. Cut the fish fillets into large slices. Sprinkle with salt.
2. Mix together scallions, ginger, soy sauce, vinegar, sherry and sugar.
3. Place some sliced ham and sliced mushrooms on each piece of fish, pour the sauce over and steam for about 15-20 minutes.

Serves 3-4.

Shrimp with Bean Sprouts

½ lb (250 g) shelled shrimp
4 tablespoons sherry
4 tablespoons vegetable oil
1 teaspoon salt
½ lb (250 g) bean sprouts
2½ tablespoons soy sauce
½ teaspoon sugar

1. De-vein the shrimp and marinate in the sherry for two hours, tossing occasionally.
2. Drain the shrimp and fry in the heated oil for about three minutes with the salt.
3. Add the bean sprouts and cook for another minute.
4. Mix in the soy sauce and sugar and serve immediately.

Serves 3-4.

Lobster Chop Suey

½ lb (250 g) cooked lobster
  meat
1 onion
¼ lb (125 g) bamboo shoots
1 stalk celery
¼ cucumber
4 medium mushrooms
¼ lb (125 g) bean sprouts

4 tablespoons oil
salt and pepper
½ cup (125 ml) chicken stock
2½ tablespoons cornstarch
1 teaspoon sugar
2½ tablespoons sherry
few drops sesame oil
2½ tablespoons soy sauce

1. Cut lobster into bite-size pieces.
2. Slice all the vegetables and saute in the oil for two minutes.
3. Add the salt, pepper and stock, cover and cook for one minute over a medium heat.
4. Mix in lobster pieces.
5. Mix the cornstarch with a little water and add to the vegetable and lobster mixture with the sugar, sherry and sesame oil. Cook for another minute or two.
6. Add the soy sauce, mix thoroughly and cook for a further minute. Serve immediately.

Serves 4.

Shrimp and Artichoke Hearts

2 lb (1 kg) raw shrimp	3 slices fresh ginger
2 teaspoons sugar	8 canned artichoke hearts
2½ tablespoons oil	2 teaspoons cornstarch
1 teaspoon salt	2½ tablespoons soy sauce

1. Shell and de-vein the shrimp. Rinse quickly under running water. Slice in half lengthwise.
2. Place shrimp in a saucepan with enough water to cover. Add sugar and simmer for ten minutes. Remove and drain.
3. Heat oil in a frypan. Add salt, ginger and shrimp. Cook for two minutes.
4. Cut artichoke hearts in quarters and add to the shrimp with the cornstarch and soy sauce. Cook for 2-3 minutes and serve immediately.

Serves 4-6.

Crab Balls

    1 lb (500 g) crabmeat
    salt
    2 egg whites
    oil for frying
    2½ tablespoons soy sauce
    pepper

1. Chop the crabmeat finely. Season with salt.
2. Beat egg whites until stiff and mix with the crabmeat.
3. Drop by the teaspoonful into hot oil and cook until golden brown on all sides. Drain on absorbent paper.
4. Sprinkle soy sauce over the crab balls. Season with a little pepper and serve immediately.

Serves 4-6.

Fried Scallops

1 lb (500 g) scallops
4 tablespoons oil
1 slice fresh ginger, chopped
6 spring onions, chopped
½ cucumber, chopped

2½ tablespoons white wine
few drops sesame oil
salt and pepper
2 teaspoons flour

1. Slice the scallops and saute in the oil for about five minutes. Remove from pan.
2. In the same frypan saute the ginger, onions and cucumber.
3. Stir in the scallops, wine, sesame oil, salt and pepper to taste and flour. Heat thoroughly and serve immediately.

Serves 3-4.

Eggs with Crabmeat

6 eggs, separated
2½ cups (625 ml) milk
¼ lb (125 g) ham
3 spring onions
⅓ cup (85 ml) oil

¼ cup flour
¼ lb (125 g) crabmeat
salt and pepper
1½ tablespoons sherry

1. Beat the egg yolks with ½ cup milk.
2. Chop the ham and the onions. Heat the oil in a saucepan and saute the ham and onions over a low heat until the onions are transparent.
3. Stir in the flour and the remaining two cups of milk.
4. Add the crabmeat and salt and pepper to taste.
5. Very slowly pour in the egg yolk mixture and the sherry.
6. Beat the egg whites until stiff and gently fold into the crabmeat mixture.
7. Pour the entire mixture into a well-buttered dish and bake in a 350°F (180°C) oven for about an hour.

Serves 6.

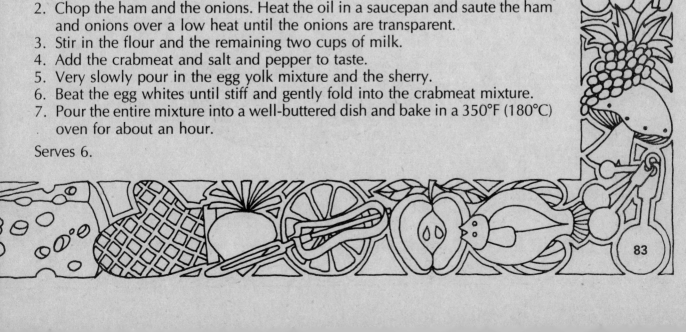

Spicy Fried Shrimp

1 lb (500 g) raw shrimp
oil for deep frying
2 scallions, chopped
1 teaspoon grated ginger
1½ tablespoons sherry
4 tablespoons oil

1½ tablespoons brown bean
sauce
1½ tablespoons tomato sauce
2 teaspoons soy sauce
½ teaspoon salt

1. Peel and de-vein the shrimp. Rinse quickly under running water. Drain and dry. Cut into two or three pieces.
2. Deep fry the shrimp until they turn red. Remove and and set aside.
3. Heat the four tablespoons of oil and saute the scallions and ginger for one minute.
4. Add shrimp and saute for another minute.
5. Add sherry and a mixture of the brown bean sauce, tomato sauce, soy sauce and salt. Cook over a high heat, stirring constantly until cooked.

Serves 3-4.

Raw Fish

½ lb (250 g) very fresh fillets
of fish
10 spring onions
½ lettuce

1½ tablespoons finely chopped
fresh ginger
2½ tablespoons oil
2½ tablespoons soy sauce

1. Rinse the fish in cold water and dry thoroughly. Cut into thin slices.
2. Chop the spring onions and the lettuce.
3. Mix together the spring onions and ginger in a large mixing bowl.
4. Heat the oil until very hot and pour over the fish mixture. Mix well.
5. Stir in the soy sauce and lettuce and serve.

Serves 2.

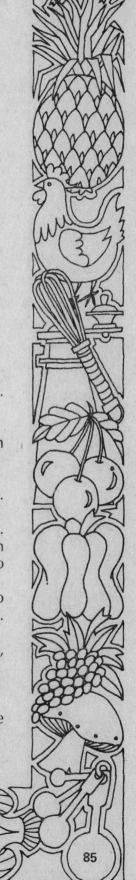

Fish Chow Mein

½ lb (250 g) fine egg noodles
1 lb (500 g) white fish fillets
3 slices fresh ginger, crushed
1½ tablespoons soy sauce
1½ tablespoons oil
½ small cauliflower
6 dried mushrooms (soaked, liquid reserved)
1 medium carrot
2 eggs
1 teaspoon salt

oil for frying
2 teaspoons salt
2½ tablespoons mushroom liquid
2 teaspoons salt
4 teaspoons cornstarch
2 teaspoons soy sauce
¼ teaspoon sugar
½ cup mushroom liquid
½ teaspoon sesame oil
pinch pepper

1. Cook the noodles in boiling salted water for one minute, stirring constantly. Drain and rinse under cold water. Set aside.
2. Cut the fish into 1-inch (2½-cm) squares.
3. Mix together the crushed ginger, soy sauce and oil and marinate the fish in this mixture for 15 minutes.
4. Cut the cauliflower, mushrooms and carrot into thin slices.
5. Beat the eggs with the one teaspoon of salt and cook like an omelette. Remove from pan and cut into strips.
6. Heat ½ cup oil in a frypan. When very hot, add the noodles. Do not stir. Allow the noodles to form into a firm cake. Cook for about three minutes on each side. Remove from pan and drain on absorbent paper. Sprinkle with two teaspoons of salt.
7. Saute the carrot, cauliflower and mushrooms for two minutes. Add the two tablespoons mushroom liquid and two teaspoons salt. Cook for one minute. Pour over the noodles.
8. Mix together the cornstarch, soy sauce, sugar, ½ cup mushroom liquid, sesame oil and pepper.
9. Saute the fish in three tablespoons hot oil.
10. Add the sauce and cook until the sauce thickens.
11. Pour the fish mixture over the noodles and vegetables. Garnish with the omelette strips.

Serves 4.

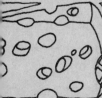

Shrimp Curry

1 lb (500 g) shelled shrimp	1½ tablespoons sherry
½ egg white	2½ tablespoons chicken stock
½ teaspoon salt	curry powder to taste
1 teaspoon cornstarch	½ teaspoon sugar
oil for deep frying	¼ teaspoon salt
1½ tablespoons oil	

1. De-vein the shrimp and rinse quickly under running water. Drain and dry.
2. Mix together the egg white, salt and cornstarch. Dip the shrimp into this mixture and deep fry until almost cooked. Remove from oil.
3. Heat the one and a half tablespoon oil in a frypan. Add the shrimp and stir in the sherry.
4. Mix together the chicken stock, curry powder, sugar and salt. Add to the shrimp and mix thoroughly. Serve immediately.

Serves 4.

Shrimp with Broccoli

1 lb (500 g) shelled shrimp	2½ tablespoons chicken stock
1 lb (500 g) broccoli	2½ tablespoons oyster sauce
oil for deep frying	1 teaspoon salt
2 cloves garlic, crushed	¼ teaspoon sugar
3 slices fresh ginger	¼ teaspoon sesame oil
1½ tablespoons sherry	pinch pepper

1. De-vein the shrimp and rinse quickly under running water. Drain and dry. Slice along back without cutting through.
2. Cook broccoli in boiling salted water for about 7 minutes. Drain.
3. Deep fry the shrimp until cooked. Drain and set aside.
4. Heat a little oil and saute the garlic and ginger for one minute. Add broccoli and shrimp and stir in the sherry.
5. Mix together the stock, oyster sauce, salt, sugar, sesame oil and pepper. Add to the shrimp and broccoli and mix well.

Serves 6.

Curried Shrimp

2 onions
2½ tablespoons oil
curry powder to taste
2 teaspoons soy sauce
½ lb (250 g) peeled shrimp
½ cup (125 ml) milk

1. Slice the onions and saute in the hot oil until golden brown.
2. Thoroughly blend in the curry powder and soy sauce.
3. De-vein the shrimp. Mix in the shrimp and milk and cook for five minutes.

Serves 2-3.

Sole in Egg Sauce

1½ lb (750 g) fillet of sole (or
   other white fish)
3 eggs
1½ teaspoons salt
¼ cup cornstarch
⅓ cup (85 ml) oil

3 scallions, finely chopped
3 slices fresh ginger, finely
   chopped
2½ tablespoons sherry
2½ tablespoons water

1. Cut the fish fillets into bite-size pieces.
2. Lightly beat the eggs with ½ teaspoon salt. Gradually mix in the cornstarch. Stir until smooth.
3. Thoroughly coat the fish pieces with the egg mixture.
4. Saute the fish in the very hot oil. Cook until golden brown.
5. Add the remainder of the salt, scallions, ginger, sherry and water to the egg mixture. Mix well. Add to the fish and cook for about five minutes.

Serves 4-6.

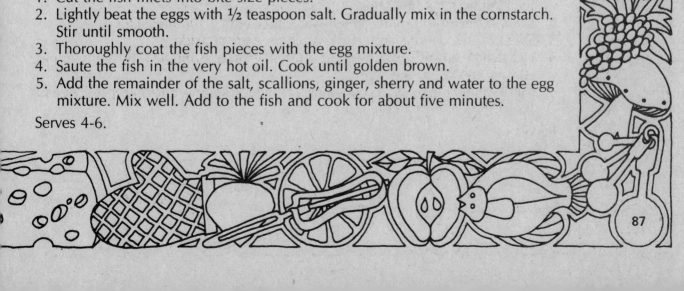

Braised Fish

2 teaspoons grated ginger	2½ tablespoons oil
1 teaspoon sugar	1 whole fish (500 g - 1 lb)
1½ tablespoons soy sauce	½ teaspoon pepper
1½ tablespoons sherry	4 tablespoons chopped
1 teaspoon salt	parsley
⅓ cup (85 ml) water	3 scallions, chopped

1. Mix together the ginger and the sugar. Then add the soy sauce, sherry, salt and water.
2. Heat the oil in a frypan and brown the fish on both sides.
3. Add the soy sauce mixture, cover and braise fish for ten minutes.
4. Remove fish from frypan and place on a dish that will fit in a large saucepan.
5. Sprinkle pepper, parsley and scallions on top of the fish.
6. Place dish on a rack above a little boiling water in a saucepan. Cover and steam for about ten minutes.

Serves 2-4.

Desserts

Sweet Pao Tsen

2 teaspoons dried yeast
1¼ cups (300 ml) warm water
3 cups plain flour
½ lb (250 g) chopped walnuts
   and almonds
⅓ cup sugar
2½ tablespoons honey
4 teaspoons butter

1. Dissolve the yeast in warm water.
2. Mix with the flour and knead into a dough. Place in an oiled bowl, cover and leave in a warm place until twice its original size (about 3-4 hours).
3. Divide into twelve equal portions and roll each into round shapes about 3 inches (8 cm) across and ½ inch (1 cm) thick. Set aside.
4. Make the filling by mixing together the chopped nuts, sugar, honey and butter.
5. Place a little of the filling in the centre of each round. Gather the outside edges together and pinch to secure.
6. Place the buns in a steamer and steam for about 20 minutes.

Serves 4-6.

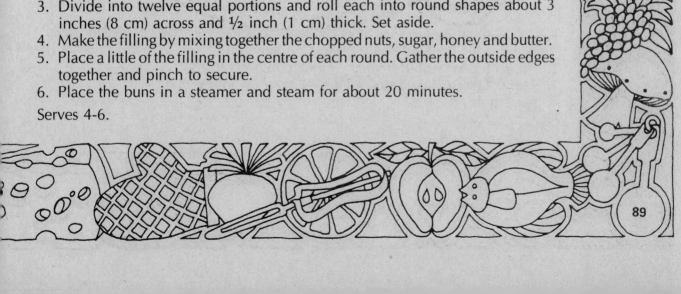

Fruit Rice Pudding

2 cups rice	½ lb (250 g) dates
5 cups (1¼ liters) water	20 kumquats
½ cup caster sugar	⅓ cup raisins
½ lb (250 g) candied fruits	20 blanched almonds

1. Simmer the rice in 3½ cups of the water until almost soft.
2. Add the sugar and the rest of the water and simmer for another 15 minutes.
3. Butter the inside of a large pudding bowl and place some of the candied fruits, dates, kumquats, raisins and nuts on the bottom in a pattern.
4. Add about 2 inches (5 cm) of rice and then another layer of the fruits and nuts. Repeat layers finishing with a layer of rice.
5. Cover with waxed paper and steam for about two hours.
6. Turn out onto a serving dish. Serve hot.

Serves 6-8.

Pears with Honey

6 pears
2 teaspoons honey for each
     pear
½ teaspoon cinnamon for each
     pear
2 teaspoons raisins for each
     pear

1. Cut off about 1 inch (2½ cm) of the stalk end of the pear. (Do not peel the pear.) Remove the core without breaking the skin.
2. Fill each pear with the honey, cinnamon and raisins.
3. Replace the tops and steam for ½-1 hour or until soft.
4. Serve hot.

Serves 6.

Almond Dessert

  1¼ cups (300 ml) evaporated
    milk
4 tablespoons sugar
3¾ cups (925 ml) water
2½ tablespoons gelatin
2½ tablespoons cold water
1 teaspoon almond essence

1. Mix together the milk, sugar and water in a saucepan and heat until the sugar dissolves. Do not allow to boil.
2. Mix the gelatin with the cold water in a large bowl. Pour the hot liquid over the gelatin mixture and stir until the gelatin is dissolved.
3. Stir in the almond essence.
4. Pour into a shallow tin and, when cool, refrigerate until set. Cut into small squares before serving.

Serves 4-6.

Lychees in Syrup

  ½ cup sugar
1¼ cups (300 ml) water
1 lb (500 g) lychees, peeled

1. Mix together the sugar and the water in a saucepan and heat until the sugar melts. Remove from heat and cool.
2. Soak the lychees in the syrup for at least ½ hour before serving.

(Fresh lychees are better, but canned lychees may also be used.)

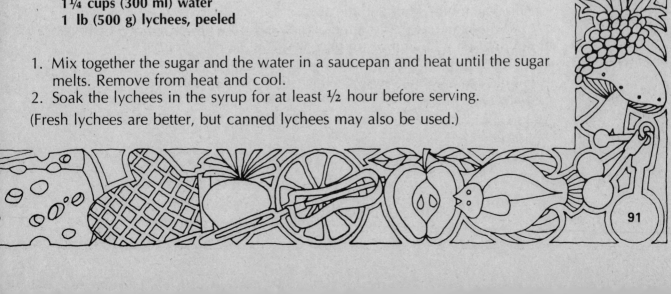

Sponge Cake

4 eggs
1 cup sugar
4 tablespoons oil
4 tablespoons milk
1 teaspoon baking powder
1½ cups flour
pinch salt

1. Beat together the eggs and the sugar until thick and light yellow in color.
2. Add the oil and milk and mix well.
3. Sift the flour, baking powder and salt and gradually add to the egg mixture. Stir well until smooth.
4. Pour into a prepared 9-inch (23-cm) cake tin. Place the tin a large saucepan and let the tin stand on a rack above the water. Cover the saucepan and steam the cake for about ½ hour.

Sesame Cookies

2 cups plain flour
½ cup sugar
½ cup (125 g) butter or
    margarine
3 teaspoons water
1 teaspoon sesame oil
1 egg
sesame seeds

1. Sift together the flour and the sugar.
2. Add the butter, water, sesame oil and egg and mix well.
3. Roll out on a floured board until very thin ⅛ inch (3 mm).
4. Cut into round cookies about 2 inches (5 cm) in diameter.
5. Firmly press sesame seeds on one side.
6. Bake in a 350°F (180°C) for ten minutes.

Makes about 2 dozen.

Peking Dust

1 lb (500 g) chestnuts
2½ tablespoons brown sugar
1 cup (250 ml) water
1 cup (250 ml) cream
2½ tablespoons caster sugar

1. Cut a criss-cross on the top of each chestnut. Put them in a saucepan and cover with water. Bring to a boil and cook for about ½ hour. Drain and shell.
2. Combine brown sugar and water in a saucepan. Add the shelled chestnuts, cover and cook over a very low heat for about ½ hour-45 minutes. Drain (if necessary) and cool.
3. Grind the chestnuts to a fine "dust". Spoon into mounds in six separate dessert dishes.
4. Whip the cream and the caster sugar together and spoon on top of chestnut dust.

Serves 6.

Honeyed Apples

6 cooking apples
¾ teaspoon salt
5½ tablespoons plain flour
5½ tablespoons cake
   flour
2 eggs
oil for deep frying
7 tablespoons oil
7 tablespoons honey
4 tablespoons sesame seeds

1. Peel the apples, cut into eighths and remove the core. Sprinkle with salt.
2. Mix together the plain flour, cake flour, eggs and 4 tablespoons water.
3. Dip the apples in the batter making very sure that the wedge is completely covered. Deep fry for about three minutes. Remove and drain on absorbent paper.
4. Heat the seven tablespoons of oil with the honey. Mix well.
5. Dip the apples in the oil and honey mixture. Remove and sprinkle with sesame seeds.

Serves 6.

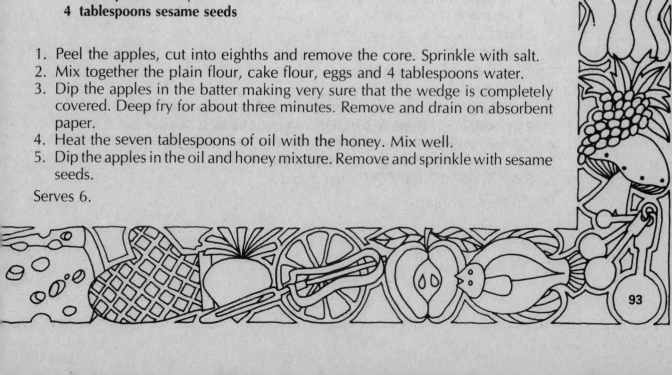

Crystallized Bananas

6 firm bananas
3 tablespoons oil
1½ teaspoons sugar
1 cup (250 ml) vinegar
¾ cup brown sugar

¼ cup cornstarch
1 teaspoon fresh ginger, chopped
¾ teaspoon salt
iced water

1. Peel the bananas and cut in half lengthwise.
2. Heat the oil and sugar in a frypan. Saute the bananas over a low heat until golden brown. Remove frypan from heat and set aside with the bananas remaining in the frypan.
3. Mix together the vinegar, brown sugar, cornstarch, ginger and salt in a saucepan and slowly bring to a boil, stirring constantly. Boil for two minutes.
4. Pour over the bananas and cook over a low heat for another two minutes.
5. Remove the bananas one by one and dip into the iced water to set the caramel coating. Serve immediately.

Serves 6.

Index

Curried Shrimp   87

Deep Fried Chicken Livers 65

Egg and Scallop Soup 18
Egg Flower Soup 10
Egg Fu Yong 59
Eggplant 36
Eggs with Crabmeat 83

Fish and Egg Flower Soup 11
Fish Chow Mein 85
Fish with Vegetables 80
Fresh Mushrooms 40
Fried Bean Sprouts 48
Fried Celery 38
Fried Fish in Sweet and Sour Sauce 79
Fried Kidney 51
Fried Liver 54
Fried Noodles with Chicken 29
Fried Noodles with Vegetables 27
Fried Noodles 28
Fried Pork and Vegetables 78
Fried Rice with Chicken 26
Fried Rice with Shrimp   26
Fried Scallops 83
Fried Scallion Cakes   36
Fried Sliced Chicken 60
Fruit Rice Pudding 90

Honeyed Apples 93
Hong Kong Rice 28

Lemon Chicken 63
Lettuce and Fish Soup 12
Lettuce and Fish Soup 22
Lobster Chop Suey 81
Lychees in Syrup 91

Marrow in Cream Sauce 48
Mixed Vegetables 41
Mixed Vegetables Soup 15
Mushrooms and Cauliflower 37
Mushrooms in White Sauce 45
Mushroom Soup 17

Noodles with Lobster 31
Noodles with Meat 30
Noodles with Pork and Water Chestnuts 30

Pears with Honey 90
Peking Dust 93
Pork and Cucumber 76
Pork Soup 20
Pork with Peanuts and Peppers 75
Pork with Walnuts 74
Pork with Peanuts 77

Quick Fried Beef with Peppers 55

Raw Fish 84
Rice with Chicken Sauce 32
Rice with Pork and Corn 31

Savoury Stuffing 23
Sesame Cookies 92
Short Soup 11
Shrimp Curry   86
Shrimp and Artichoke Hearts   82
Shrimp with Broccoli 86
Shrimp with Bean Sprouts 81
Sole in Egg Sauce 87
Sour Soup 20
Special Stirred Rice 24
Spicy Fried Shrimp 84
Spinach and Shrimp 44
Spicy Fried Prawns 84
Spinach and Prawns 44
Spinach with Minced Pork 46
Spring Rolls 73
Sponge Cake 92
Steamed Bread 23
Steamed Fish Sliced 80
Steamed Rice 25
Stirred Rice 39
Stuffed Peppers 44
Stuffed Peppers 49
Sweet and Sour Carrots 35
Sweet and Sour Pork 72
Sweet and Sour Pork with
    Pineapple and Peppers 74
Sweet and Sour Pork Spareribs 75
Sweet and Sour Radishes 40
Sweet Pao Tsen 89
Sweet Stuffing 23

Vegetable Fried Rice 33

Watercress Soup 14

FR-B8096-3/69